TRIGGER UNIT

USING HEALTH AND ILLNESS TO UNDERSTAND SOCIAL PSYCHOLOGICAL PROBLEMS AND PERSPECTIVES

by Jeannette Murphy

Contents

Introduction

In this Trigger Unit you will be asked to adopt the role of a social psychologist and to think about the sorts of problems you might want to investigate, and the types of questions you might want to ask about personal experience and social life. You will also be exposed to two important organizing principles of the course: the different domains within which social psychologists operate and the diverse perspectives they use. In order to gain experience in using the tools and concepts of the discipline you need *material* (in the form of examples and data) on which you will be able to practise your analytical and observational skills. The function of the Trigger Unit is to provide you with this material.

Ideally, the focus of this practice material should be familiar to you and at the same time rich and complex enough to ensure that it can be viewed from a variety of perspectives and across different domains. The topic we have selected to get you started thinking about what is involved in social psychology is *health and illness*. The potential of this topic as a device for triggering you to practise social psychology is explored later in this introduction.

Aims of Trigger Unit

The Trigger Unit is meant to get you thinking about the nature and scope of social psychology before you read the four course books. It seeks to arouse your curiosity, to make you puzzle over the mundane as well as the unusual features of your social world. We hope that it will help you to develop your powers of observation.

The Trigger Unit should also prepare you for the way in which the rest of the course is structured and its underlying premises. In particular, it should make you aware that social psychology does *not* operate with a single theoretical perspective. You will discover that what characterizes the discipline is *diversity*. Social psychologists employ a variety of theoretical perspectives to make sense of personal lives and social worlds. And the methods they use to study social psychological phenomena are equally diverse. Finally, the topics they choose to study are drawn from three different domains: the individual person, the interpersonal and the socio-cultural.

The Trigger Unit aims to:

- encourage you to think about the way in which social psychologists construct research problems
- highlight the three domains across which social psychologists typically operate: the individual person, the interpersonal, and the group or social collective
- alert you to the multiperspective nature of social psychology
- get you thinking about the research strategies employed by social psychologists and the types of data collected

- challenge you to look critically at popular accounts of social behaviour and social life
- highlight the way in which social psychology borrows from and overlaps with other disciplines (e.g. sociology, anthropology)
- motivate you to reflect on the value of personal experience in helping you to make sense of social psychology.

Why have a Trigger Unit?

A *trigger* is something which starts or initiates a process; it acts as a stimulus. We commonly speak about a word or action 'triggering off' other thoughts or actions. This unit is meant to trigger a process of reflection — to get you to explore your social world, test your observations, and reflect on the way you make sense of social events.

When studying for a degree, especially in the social sciences, it is very useful to have opportunities to discuss and to argue, to listen to debates, to take part in dialogues — not just with a tutor but with other students. This is the reason why so many courses schedule seminars as a place for hearing and discussing other points of view. Although a written text cannot substitute for this live exchange of ideas, the Trigger Unit seeks to initiate conversations in your head. That is, it seeks to provoke you into examining your own views, exploring your values and your implicit assumptions. If the Trigger Unit succeeds in this goal, you will also want to hold these conversations with friends, family, and colleagues to find out what they think and to test out your ideas on them.

We, the course team, realize that we are writing for students who bring to the course a tremendously varied set of social experiences. You will each have your preferred way of looking at the world, of interpreting your social encounters. In some cases, these models of social psychology may be very deep or implicit; you may not even be aware that you are operating with assumptions or preconceptions.

This poses a challenge to us and to you. How do we guide you through the literature and theories of academic social psychology? How do we assist you to draw on social psychological methods and perspectives to make sense of your social world? Do we turn a blind eye to the fact that you are actors in the social world, with your own scripts, your own orientation to social life? Or do we try to work with your prior knowledge and experience? Do we try to help you to uncover your world view and get you to reflect upon it, to build upon it? We've chosen the latter course and for this reason you will begin your study of D317 by examining what you know about the social world, by testing the limits of your understanding of social life in the area of health and illness.

Essentially, this unit will consist of a series of triggers (e.g. scenarios, extracts, summaries, challenges) which you will be invited to read, respond to and discuss with others. Quite often you will be given feedback (this is not the same as correct 'answers'). For you to benefit from this Trigger Unit you will need to leave yourself time to interact with the material.

The three domains of social psychology

D317 is divided into three main books. Each book deals with one of the domains within which social psychology operates.

- Book 1 focuses on issues to do with individuals; it raises questions about what it means to be a person.

- Book 2 explores issues to do with social interactions and personal relationships.

- Book 3 reviews issues concerning groups, collectivities and institutions (the sociocultural domain).

In addition, there is a fourth book, *Issues for Social Psychology,* in which the conceptual matters and theoretical tensions that cut across the other three books are discussed.

The organization of the Trigger Unit mirrors the way in which the course as a whole is structured. So we begin in the first section by asking how human beings experience health and illness at a personal, individual level. For example, how do we make sense of illness? What does it mean to an individual person to be healthy or to feel healthy? As you will see, a number of distinct perspectives can be used to study issues in this domain.

Our second section focuses on the social interactions which develop around health and illness. Discussion centres on two situations: the interactions which occur between individual patients and healthcare professionals and the relationship that is formed between informal carers and persons who receive care. You will also be introduced to some of the methods used to study social relationships and interactions.

The third section of this unit looks at the ways in which culture and society affect health and illness. Out of the many possible topics we could examine here, we have selected three issues: the socialization of healthcare professions, cultural representations of health and illness, and tension in the healthcare system.

The topics selected from the field of health and illness to illustrate these three domains are certainly not exhaustive; there is much more that could be examined in relation to each. If you have a particular interest in issues to do with health and illness, you should have opportunities to return to this topic at various points in the course, for example in your projects or your TMAs.

It is important to clarify a few points about organizing the course around these three domains. At first glance, it may appear that there is a hierarchy — that some domains are more important or more basic or that some are higher or more complex. However, once you begin to study the books, you will seen that this is not the message of the course. Crosscutting the domains are perspectives which are not specific to any single domain. For example, one of the perspectives is the biological perspective which is used to explain phenomena within all three domains: the individual, the interpersonal and the sociocultural domain. You will meet biologically-oriented accounts of addiction behaviour; you will also encounter theories of interpersonal attraction which suggest that genetic programming may play a role in our choice of partners.

All three domains (individual, relationships, and socio-cultural) coexist and need to be taken into account when doing social psychology. As people we do not only need to operate as individuals, we also need to participate in small, intimate groups, and to partake in the wider society. Each domain enters into our way of experiencing and making sense of our personal lives. What the course seeks to demonstrate is that, although it is analytically possible to focus on issues which are specific to a particular domain, as soon as we start to examine an issue situated in one domain, we find that it is impossible to totally exclude the other domains. For instance, in exploring the way in which *individuals* experience illness, we need to know something about their social support networks and their cultural background.

Despite the fact that the domains are not self-contained realms, from the point of view of an individual, there may well be moments or episodes when one set of issues *seems* more important, more dominant, more controlling or more central.

ACTIVITY I

How do we experience the three domains?

Can you think of occasions when issues relating to one domain seem to dominate, pushing the others to the background?

When might the individual, personal domain overshadow the other two?

When might the interpersonal domain seem most significant?

Are there ever times when the social, cultural, economic, political domain seems to exert the major influence?

Feedback is given in the 'Feedback for Activities' section on page 101 of this unit.

In addition to this question of the interrelationship between the three domains, there are other questions which this way of structuring the course may raise in your mind. For instance, is there continuity across the three domains (the person, interpersonal relations and social groups) in terms of key questions, concepts, methods, metaphors or theories? Is it possible for social psychology to operate across three such different domains?

At this stage we will not attempt to answer these questions. But you will be invited to think about these issues as you progress through the course. And as you read the core books you will be directed by the Study Guide, at relevant points, to Book 4 where questions to do with philosophy, discipline boundaries and methods will be debated. This will give you the opportunity to look in greater detail at the divisions and tensions which characterize social psychology.

What will become apparent as you study D317 is that, in order to tackle issues which span the three domains, social psychologists have needed to be eclectic, and have borrowed from many fields e.g. from psychology, anthropology, sociology, philosophy and biology. But this very breadth of theoretical concepts and research methods may appear to produce some confusion of identity. As the discipline has grown, the very phrase *social psychology* (in the singular) has come to seem a misnomer; given the diversity of approaches, it may be more accurate to speak of *social psychologies*! If you were to browse through a few social psychology textbooks in your local library or bookshop, you would find that the contents of D317 do not necessarily correspond to the headings in other books. This is partly a matter of presentational style and partly a reflection of the fact that, rather than seeking to impose unity on the subject matter, D317 acknowledges and explores the diverse (and sometimes contradictory) strands of modern social psychology.

A multiperspective approach to social psychology

D317 is deliberately open-ended about what social psychology is. Instead of providing you with a clear-cut statement as to what social psychology *is*, where its boundaries lie, what its central problems are, D317 takes these questions to be at the heart of contemporary debate about what it means to *do* or to study social psychology. Consequently, the course is designed to expose you to different voices. Throughout the course you will be invited to think about the type of knowledge which different perspectives provide. An allied issue is who has the power to define the subject matter, the methods and the theoretical models of the discipline. Why have we chosen to produce a course which embraces diversity? The course team designed the course in this way because we felt it best reflects where social psychology has got to at the end of the twentieth century. Far from being a monolithic discipline dominated by a single perspective, social psychology is more like a kaleidoscope in which the constituent elements reassemble themselves into different patterns as you change your angle of vision.

So not only will you need to think about the three different domains, but in the course of your journey through D317, you will also be introduced to quite distinct theoretical perspectives. Although each of the three books adopts a multiperspective approach, Book 1, in particular, is structured in such a way that you can readily see the way in which five different perspectives go about making sense of what it means to be a person in a social world. The five perspectives are discussed in more detail in relation to the topic of health and illness in section 1.6 of the Trigger Unit.

Book 1 gives you the opportunity to compare the way in which perspectives as varied as biology and psychodynamic theory can be brought to bear on problems relating to personhood. Likewise, Book 2 adopts a pluralist stance and shows how the topics of social interactions and personal relationships have been theorized and researched by social psychologists working within quite different perspectives. You will meet again some of the perspectives first introduced in Book 1 as well as others which seem to have a natural affinity with the interpersonal domain. In the final book of the course most of the perspectives you meet will be familiar from the first two books. You will see how perspectives (e.g. social constructionism) which have been applied within the domain of the individual are also relevant to issues arising within the sociocultural domain.

What does this diversity mean for you, the student? A course which builds upon a multiperspective foundation demands that students do more than simply learn facts or focus on content; it is important to look beyond the results or claims of different social psychologists and to think about the *process* by which they have created their insights, or assembled their evidence. You need to think about the meaning or the status of the findings made by individuals operating with quite different perspectives. Does this sound daunting? It is a big challenge, but you will be given support to help you cope with the tensions you experience as you make the transition from one perspective to another. In particular, Book 4 has been designed to address the question of diversity which lies at the heart of D317. It will provide you with a chance to stand aside from the content matter of particular chapters and to reflect on ways of dealing with the diversity which you will meet in the books. In addition, the interrelationship between these different perspectives will be a recurrent theme within each of the books. Chapter authors will suggest ways of locating different perspectives and you will be exposed to different ideas on how to cope with the fact that social psychology is not a unified discipline.

Health and illness as the focal point of the Trigger Unit

What may at first strike you as odd about this Trigger Unit is that you are *not* primarily studying it in order to pick up 'content'. So when you are reading this unit bear in mind that you are not required to learn a whole body of knowledge called 'health and illness' or 'health psychology'. Although we will be looking at the topic of health and illness, don't be misled into thinking that the Trigger Unit offers a comprehensive account of the social psychology of health and illness (there is an enormous literature on this *per se*). Instead, this unit is a selection of research which has been chosen to link to the storyline of the course. Therefore, it does not reflect the full range of theories or research traditions which you will find in a textbook on health psychology. (If you are interested in doing further reading in this field, you will find suggested readings on pages 71 and 114 of this unit.)

The material assembled here is intended to help you to see how different social psychological perspectives can be brought to bear on the topic of health and illness, to prepare you to identify and define problems which you think it would be worthwhile studying, and to make you aware of the fact that one's initial perspective will play a significant role in identifying problems and deciding how to study them. *This is not to imply, however, that the content of the unit is unimportant or irrelevant.* While you will not be directly assessed on the content of the Trigger Unit you can bring this material, where relevant, into your assessments. Furthermore, the skills and the method of approach we are seeking to foster in the Trigger Unit will help you succeed in the rest of the course.

A note on terminology

One of the confusing things at the outset of any new course is the vocabulary used by the various authors and the nuances of meaning attached to particular words. In D317 there is a set of core terms which run throughout the course which will be analysed and debated in Book 4. But to get you started here are some of the key concepts:

- *discipline*: a branch of knowledge, e.g. psychology, sociology, history (sometimes called a subject)
- *domain*: a way of dividing up a discipline into fields of thought or action
- *perspective:* a way of approaching a discipline; a set of overarching assumptions
- *theory:* a system of ideas for explaining something.

How do these concepts map on to one another? The first thing to note is that for some purposes we may choose to consider social psychology as a discipline in its own right and in other contexts it may be presented as a domain of psychology (and of sociology). In turn, we may group disciplines such as psychology, anthropology and sociology together under the heading social sciences. The key point is that any discipline is associated with a variety of domains and domains may link to more than one discipline.

If we treat social psychology as a discipline, then, for the purpose of D317, it is linked to three domains, and, at the same time, it is also connected to a variety of perspectives. Again, these perspectives are not necessarily unique to a single discipline or a single domain. The perspectives represented in D317 may be used in general psychology and in other social sciences. A perspective can, in turn, be the nodal point for several theories.

How to use the Trigger Unit

An important function of the Trigger Unit is to provide opportunities for you to start developing your own view of social psychology which you can refine as you study the rest of the course material. As you study D317 you will come to realize that social psychology is not a finished product; it is not a fixed body of knowledge, insights and methods. Rather, it is an evolving discipline which is reshaped by each new generation of social theorists and researchers. The course itself represents a new way of approaching the study of social psychology. As mentioned earlier, D317 encompasses a variety of perspectives and it requires you to be alert to the implications of the claims made by those working within different perspectives.

The best way for you to appreciate that the discipline boundaries are not rigid and that there are multiple perspectives contained within this subject called social psychology, is for you to produce accounts or explanations of your experiences and observations, and to compare *your* way of making sense with that of other students, or your tutors or authorities in the field. (You will have an activity along these lines in the next section of the Trigger Unit.)

As you become acquainted with the diversity of points of view held by different groups of social psychologists, you will understand why it is impossible to point to one author or one textbook or one school of thought and say that this author, textbook or school of thought encapsulates social psychology at the end of the twentieth century.

What will be expected of you?

The Trigger Unit is designed to be an interactive form of study. It is not based exclusively on reading what experts have to say nor will it teach you about results or statistical methods or different world views. Instead the unit will require you to reflect, find out and talk to other people.

Throughout the unit you will be asked to reflect on your experiences and the way in which you make sense of what you see and feel. If you are to benefit from the course as a whole, it is important that you set aside time to contemplate your world and the skills, knowledge and interpretations which allow you to interact with other people. Your task will be to find a way of assimilating the contents of D317 and integrating it with your prior knowledge and experience.

While in the other parts of this course you will be asked to read source material, to consider evidence and to undertake various activities, in this unit the focus for much of the time will be on *your* experience — what you as an individual bring with you to D317. And because of the open-ended nature of the problems you will be asked to explore, there will not be simple 'right' answers. Instead, you will be provided with illustrations or you may be asked to exchange ideas with other people.

To illustrate the method which will permeate this unit, let us start by thinking about why you are doing this course. What do you hope to get out of studying social psychology?

Why study social psychology?   ACTIVITY 2

This activity asks you to provide an account of your own motives.

What do you want to get out of the course? Jot down as many reasons/ motives/accounts you *could* give for taking this course.

Do you think you would be likely to give different reasons to different people? Think about how you would explain your action to different audiences. For example:

- to your child(ren)

- to your partner

- to your employer

- to your parents

- to your tutor

- to friends

- to workmates or colleagues.

Next try to classify your reasons. Is it possible for you to rank them in terms of importance?

Now spend a few minutes reflecting on your list. Are all of these explanations 'true'? Is it possible for there to be more than one reason or motive for an action such as 'selecting an OU course'?

Is it possible that your motives for studying social psychology might change as the year progresses? Might there be factors influencing your behaviour of which you are unaware?

Thinking back over other courses you have taken, try to imagine how you might feel about D317 in a month's time, in six months' time or at the end of the course.

The point of asking you to consider your motives (the causes of your behaviour) is to provide a simple example of the complexity of human action. In the social sphere, in the world of human interaction, behaviour is likely to have more than one cause, and, over time, causes may change. It is frequently necessary to make a distinction between the factors which initiate a course of action (such as deciding to study) and the factors which sustain that behaviour over a period of time. For instance, you may decide to take social psychology because you need a course at this level to obtain your degree, and because a friend who studied social psychology told you that it was interesting and would let you borrow her books. Several months later your commitment to the course may reflect the fact that you have formed a close friendship with several other people in your tutorial group or you find your tutor is very supportive or you have discovered for yourself that the subject matter is fascinating.

Creating your own Resource File

The Trigger Unit contains extracts and activities relating to health and illness, however, we would also like to encourage you to build your own file of resources to which you could refer while you are working on this unit. If, at the end of two weeks, you find that you have enjoyed collecting this material, you may want to continue collecting material which you could use for your *Social Representations in the Media* project (an option for TMA05 in alternate years, further details of which are given on page 13.)

Here are some examples of the types of materials you could collect:

- newspaper and magazine articles about health and illness
- items in 'Problem/Advice' columns relating to health
- advertisements which seek to persuade you to buy products on the grounds that they will improve your health or prevent ill health or cure a health problem
- so-called 'grey' literature (e.g. advice/information leaflets, brochures, advertising/promotional material — the sorts of material given out in doctors' surgeries)
- commentary or reviews of television or radio programmes or films which deal with health and illness
- details of telephone advice lines which deal with health problems
- extracts from novels, poems or short stories which contain accounts of illness
- material from health promotion campaigns (leaflets, posters).

How you might use such material?

1   Relate the material to the three domains of D317

At the end of the two week period allocated to the Trigger Unit, you could review your material to try to identify the domains to which your items relate. Ask yourself whether questions, answers, or personal experience typically deal with a single domain or whether there is a tendency for the domains to blend together in commentary and analysis regarding health and illness.

2   Focus on the discourses used in the various items

See whether you can detect different 'discourses' regarding health and illness. Does there appear to be a medical or scientific way of talking about health as opposed to a more everyday language regarding health? Are there valid alternatives to official discourses? Does any of the material you have collected use discourses relating to alternative or complementary medicine?

3   Identify common themes

Try to classify your material in terms of major themes and then look for common themes that recur in the various items you have collected e.g. problems of growing old, problems of children's health, problems of men's/women's health, doctor–patient communications. Consider whether such themes or preoccupations tell us something about our society. Does your collection imply that, as a culture, we are preoccupied with health? Did you find any examples of 'health fascism'?

4   Map the material to studies in the Trigger Unit

See whether the material you've collected maps onto the studies described in the unit (in terms of methodology, assumptions or interpretations).

Compiling your Resource File

It is not intended that you spend a large amount of time on this activity. Instead, you should seek to pick up material as a by-product of your usual reading and your everyday activities. As you read through the papers or watch television or pay a visit to the chemist or your doctor, be on the lookout for useful items. You might want to paste items into a notebook or you may want to insert them into plastic files which you put into a box or into a ring binder or just put them in a box or folder. Whatever method you choose to keep your material, however, do be sure to note the date and source of each item. If you have the time, you might jot down a few ideas that occurred to you when you came across the material.

Cautionary note

This exercise is meant to stimulate you to look outside the course for *non-academic* material which focuses on health and illness. You need to be careful not to regard this as solid evidence. Such material is best used as a starting point for generating formal statements (or hypotheses) or to illustrate an argument. Although it is possible to design studies which use such material as a way of getting at cultural representations of health and illness, your selection of materials will be arbitrary and unsystematic and this means you cannot generalize from it.

TMA05 Project: Social Representations in the Media

One of the options in the media project entails looking at social representation of health and illness in the press. You may, if you wish, build on the work you have done in creating your Resource File. Note: the social representations option focuses on gender, not health and illness, in alternate years.

1 Individual experiences of health and illness

Introduction

This part of the Trigger Unit asks you to consider how individuals experience health and illness, and the ways in which they talk about their experiences. In addition, we want to consider the relationship between everyday forms of explanation and the perspectives presented in Book 1.

But before we start to have at look at some of the work which has been done in this area, it would be worthwhile spending a few minutes thinking about *why* social psychologists might want to look at individual ways of talking about health or at individual experiences of illness.

> As a social psychology student, can you think of one or two questions relating to *individual* experiences of health and illness which you feel it might be interesting to pursue? How would you justify doing research which focuses on personal experience?

1.1   The dominance of the biomedical model

In our society, health and illness issues have long been seen as being the province of doctors and others professionals with a biomedical training. Their main concern has been to understand the scientific basis of disease. Richard Baron (1985), an American doctor, spells out the consequences of the dominance of the biomedical model:

> In general, modern medicine takes disease to be an anatomicopathologic fact. We tend to see illness as an objective entity that is located somewhere anatomically ... In a profound sense, we say that such an entity 'is' the disease, thus taking illness from the universe of experience and moving it to a location in the physical world. We use object words to describe illness — lesion, tumour, infiltrate ...
>
> *(p. 606)*

One of the recurrent criticisms of the biomedical perspective is that it excludes social and psychological dimensions of ill health, and the context of illness: 'The medical perspective assumes that diseases are universal in form, progress, and content ... that is, it is assumed that tuberculosis will be the same disease, in whatever culture or society it appears.' (Helman, 1990, p. 89)

Yet it is precisely the neglected psychological, social and cultural dimensions, which Helman (1990) maintains 'determine the *meaning* of the disease for individual patients, and for those around them.' (p. 89)

There are many critics, both within the clinical world and without, who believe that there is an urgent need to take into account the way in which various illnesses are experienced, the conceptions we have about what it means to be healthy, and what we expect of medical science. The significance of this approach is that it does not separate illness from the person.

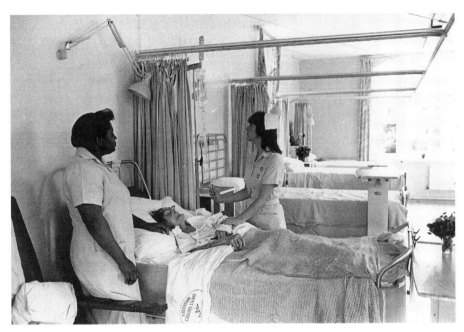

The biomedical model of illness has shaped the way in which patients are treated in hospital

If we want to capture the immediacy of what it is like to be healthy or ill, then we need something other than a biomedical approach to illness and the human body, one which brings in the concept of the *self* and the *meanings* which human beings attach to their experience. We need to explore *how* individuals react to illness. We need to probe *what* illness means in relation to personhood. The only way to answer these questions, many argue, is by listening to patients' stories. In *Worlds of Illness*, Alan Radley (1993), a British social psychologist, outlines why we need to study how people experience illness. He emphasizes the value of a biographical understanding of illness which looks at the patient's own interpretation of the onset, progress and the potential of the treatment of their condition.

1.2   Gaining insight into individual experiences of health and illness

To find out how individuals experience health and illness we need to use methods which get people to talk about their experience in an open-ended way. Although formal interviews with structured questionnaires may have a value in some research areas, if we rely exclusively on this method to determine what illness means to individuals, we are likely to force responses into a set of predetermined categories. As well as talking to people, another way of gaining insight into the meaning of illness is through literature and other cultural forms: novels, poems, auto-biographies, films, plays or television documentaries are all potential sources of material for social psychologists interested in the nature of personhood.

ACTIVITY 1.1

Before you read on, try to recall any stories, novels or biographies you have read or plays, films or television documentaries you have seen which provide an insight into how people experience illness.

Do you feel that you learned anything about the nature of individual experience from these accounts?

Resource File

Have you collected any items which give a first-hand account of health or illness?

Some of the best accounts of the way in which people live with illness have come from doctors and from patients. The neurologist, Oliver Sacks, for example, has provided us with many rich accounts of how individuals experience and live with illness. His approach stresses *the need to listen*:

> If we wish to know a man, we ask 'what is his story, his real, inmost story?', for each of us *is* a biography, a story. Each of us *is* a singular narrative, which is constructed continually and unconsciously by, through, and in us — through our perceptions, our feelings, our thoughts, our actions; and, not least, through our discourse, our spoken narrations. Biologically, physiologically, we are not so differ-ent from each other; historically, as narratives, we are each of us unique.
>
> *(Sacks, 1985, p. 12, as quoted by Brody, 1987, p. xi)*

Many of Sacks' stories about his patients relate to individuals with unusual or extreme conditions which result in the person being unable to remember his or her place in the world. Of course, in most illnesses this loss of self, of personhood, is not so dramatic. Nonetheless, there are subtle changes that occur in all sickness which cannot readily be explained at the biological level. To make sense of experiences of illness we may need to delve into 'the particular narratives of individuals and how these narratives constitute a person's life, in sickness and in health.'

Reflect briefly on your own experience of illness — be it a minor infection, a major illness, an accident or a chronic condition. Try to focus on one particular episode. How did that experience affect you as a person?

Write a few notes on how you felt about yourself when you were ill. Try to remember whether your illness had an impact on your relationship with your family or friends. Did it disrupt your sense of time or space?

ACTIVITY 1.2

1.3   The impact of illness on the self

One of the things that illness frequently does is to undermine or disturb the usual taken-for-granted relationship we have with our bodies. As Brody explains:

> ... at the level of immediate experience, I am I, a single entity, not an admixture of mind-me and body-me. My body is not a different substance, but simply my own presence in an interaction with the world. My body moving through the world and bumping into things is simply me moving and bumping. It follows from this that, if sickness leads us to see our bodies as being something foreign, thwarting our will by their intransigence and unmanageability, then sickness has fundamentally altered our experience of self and has introduced a sense of split and disruption where formerly unity reigned.
>
> *(Brody, 1987, p. 27)*

Have you or someone close to you ever had the experience of your body seeming alien to you because it was not under your control? What triggered this event? Can you recall what it felt like?

ACTIVITY 1.3

The extract from Oliver Sacks, quoted by Brody (1987) and reproduced below, provides a very vivid account of how illness may disrupt a person's relationship with their biological body and their sense of self. In the account Sacks describes his experience of nerve damage to his leg, following a fall while climbing a mountain. He recounts how his 'lived body' (which ordinarily did as bid) was turned into an 'object body' (which refused to cooperate).

Oliver Sacks, clinical neurologist and the author of 'A Leg to Stand On'. He also wrote 'Awakenings' from which the extract on Leonard in Chapter 1 of Book 1 is taken

The neurologist Oliver Sacks has written an account of his experience of breaking his leg while mountain climbing. He discovered later that he had also suffered considerable nerve damage, resulting in loss of movement and sensation and necessitating a prolonged period of recuperation. Even before he was aware of the grave extent of his injuries, Sacks describes how a disruption of self set in: 'My first thought was this: that there had been an accident, and that *someone I knew* had been seriously injured' (p. 21) Later, in the hospital, Sacks finally realized that his quadriceps muscle was paralysed; but he was also aware, with dread and foreboding, that his 'calling out' to the muscle, his 'trying' to move his muscle, constituted by its ineffectiveness a funny sort of *inability to call out or to try*. In neurological terms, he sensed a peripheral lesion but then came to relocate the lesion as a central one: *'not just a lesion in my muscle, but a lesion in me'* (p. 67)...

Later, the sensory aspect of this denervation experience hit Sacks with full force — not only could he not move his leg when he 'tried', but he could not tell without looking whether the leg was on the bed or falling off the side. Again, this peripheral phenomenon suggests experientially a central gap of existence: 'In that instant … *I knew not my leg. It was utterly strange, not-mine, unfamiliar. I gazed upon it with absolute non-recognition*' (p. 72). It is not, Sacks realizes, as if he has simply lost his leg, as if he were an amputee; in a deeper sense, he has lost the place where the leg is supposed to go; if his leg were to be returned to him he would have nowhere to put it. In short, the disruption of his sense of self and of his sense of reality is much deeper than would be suggested by 'my leg is paralyzed and I can't feel anything in it'. This experience persisted throughout a long course of physical therapy, during which the leg slowly improved. It left only when Sacks discovered himself walking automatically and unthinkingly in time to music: 'In the very moment when my "motor" music, my kinetic melody, my walking came back — in this self-same moment *the leg came back. Suddenly, with no warning, no transition whatever, the leg felt alive, and real and mine*' (p. 144).

(Source: Brody, 1987, pp. 27–28)

One lesson Brody draws from Sacks' experience is that at no time during these events was Sacks truly afraid that he would die. Death is the ultimate dissolution of self and of personhood, and it might be assumed that the experience of illness is threatening and unpleasant simply because it reminds us of our own mortality. But Sacks' observations suggest that illness is *of itself* an unpleasant disruption of the self, independent of the possibility of death.

1.4 What happens when the doctor is a patient?

The next account we examine is also autobiographical, a doctor's reflection on his own illness. While it is a personal account, it extends beyond the domain of the person because we learn about how the social organization of an intensive care unit impacts upon a patient.

In his article 'Life at the other end of the endotracheal tube: a physician's personal view of critical illness', Viner (1985) describes his own first-hand experience of intensive care. At the time of writing, the author was a 34-year-old haematologist working with critically ill and dying patients. He prefaces his account by the statement that doctors dealing with critically ill patients need to remind themselves that 'there is a living, thinking, feeling, and frightened human being on the other end of that machine' (p. 3). Viner claims that doctors do not *really* know what they ask their patients to endure; nor do they understand what a devastating physical and emotional experience it is to be critically ill. For him, as for Sacks, what illness did was to highlight the intimate relationship between body and self.

> After a time, having long since lost any ability to control the situation physically, I also began to lose emotional control. At times I was frankly psychotic. Intermittently I realized this, and was both very frightened and embarrassed by it. While intellectually I knew what was happening to me, and that it would pass if I survived, nonetheless, I became quite concerned about whether I would be whole again mentally. I also worried that I would never be able to function as a doctor again. I thought about asking to see a psychiatrist, but decided that he really could not help …
>
> (p. 9)

During his 120 day period of hospitalization for a large abdominal abscess, leading to septicaemic shock, Viner experienced delusional ideas, dreams and nightmares brought on by sleep deprivation, morphine and the intensity of his physical problems. Looking back on this experience once he had recovered, Viner notes that what characterized his experience was not so much suffering pain, which was readily relieved by morphine, but misery.

> A more important and difficult challenge was being just plain *miserable*. Under this heading I include the problem of being chronically uncomfortable, with multiple chest tubes making it impossible to move or breathe without a sharp reminder, and the raw post-tonsillectomy feeling in one's throat after a nasogastric tube has been in place for 31 straight days. Also included in the misery category are the problems of nausea, abdominal cramps, and hiccoughs, of feeling dirty, with no decent bath or shampoo for many weeks, the bad taste of an oral fungus infection and multiple other minor indispositions. Sleep deprivation was also a very difficult contributing problem for me … Time, in general, passed at a snail's pace, and most nights seemed interminable.
>
> (p. 10)

Trapped in this way, dependent on machines to breathe and other people to meet his everyday needs, the writer describes his mental struggle as to whether he wanted to live or to die. His thoughts, he tells us, became quite ambivalent. He spent much of his time thinking nostalgically about his family and about all the everyday things which one takes for granted.

Viner did recover and returned to a hospital to work as a doctor. However, his outlook on life and his relationship to his patients had been fundamentally altered. His concluding remarks sum up these alterations.

> I would like to think that my experience has helped me to be a better doctor in a number of basic ways. I hope, and trust, that I now find it easier to listen to the patient. I no longer use machines and other intensive supportive procedures simply because they exist. I am able

to talk more easily with sick people now that I have been there, and I understand that these patients are preoccupied with the fear of dying and want to talk about it. I am much more liberal with the use of morphine, when indicated, and can accept comfort as an end in itself. In short, I am able to deal better with the fact that some patients should be allowed to die quietly, with dignity, and without machines.

So, my final message is that we must not become a battery of specialists rendering superior *treatment* while *care* is absent. The patient should be the *beneficiary* of what we are doing, and not the *victim*. We must always keep our perspective, and not get lost in the maelstrom of our technology. We must always keep track of where we are going with our machines, not only medically and scientifically, but also economically, legally, morally and humanly.

(p. 13)

The account above is one person's dramatic account of intensive care: reread Viner's quotes and think about the following.

Do they provide any general insight into how individuals experience acute illness in a hospital setting?

Do you agree with Viner's reflections on the lessons for those who work in intensive care?

ACTIVITY 1.4

1.5 The value of personal accounts of health and illness

While a study of personal experience of illness may be fascinating to social psychologists interested in what it means to be a person, is such data relevant to clinicians? Viner's analysis of his own experience suggests that medical care would be improved if doctors and nurses paid attention to the patient's experiences as well as their biophysical signs and symptoms. By and large modern medicine has tended to ignore the patient's subjective experience and understanding. This comes across in the way in which medical records are written — very little is included about what patients understand and feel. Some doctors believe that listening to the patient's story and making an effort to get the voice of the patient into the history of their present illness would help to improve the relationship between healthcare professionals and patients.

Nowadays, medical narratives tend to neglect or objectify subjective experience, including symptoms. Such narratives concentrate, in the manner of chronicles, on events in the exterior, objective world rather than in the interior world of the sick. Medical students and physicians will construct more balanced accounts of human illness once they envision these accounts as 'story', a form of narrative that traditionally accesses subjective experience as well as objective events.

(Donnelly, 1988, p. 823)

Writing in the Journal of the American Medical Association, Donnelly, an American doctor, notes that what is generally recorded in the patient record is:

... little more than a chronologic arrangement of events and facts, more of a chronicle than a story. A chronicle sticks to events, to what has happened in the physical world. A story ... should tell us more, specifically, something of what has happened in the interior world of the protagonist or, in this case, the patient.

(p. 823)

ACTIVITY 1.5

The way in which healthcare professionals talk about patients

If you yourself are a healthcare professional, do you agree with Donnelly's comments? If he is right, do you think that depersonalized methods of recording make any difference to the quality of care patients receive?

Thinking back to your own training, do you have any views on the way in which you were trained to write and speak about your patients? Do you think that there are differences between different healthcare professionals in terms of the way in which they talk about patients?

Donnelly suggests that in order to understand why information regarding what the patient understands and feels about his or her diagnosis and how they are coping are excluded from casenotes, we need to examine the notion of 'taking a history'. This widely-used phrase suggests that what doctors do when they interact with patients is to simply collect some 'facts' from 'out there' which they then assemble in chronological order. Donnelly maintains, however, that *histories are made, not taken:*

Medical histories, like written histories of nations or institutions, are not taken but made. ... Furthermore, whatever we physicians compose and record as history is not 'reality' in any global sense, but one version of reality, one that we choose to construct. Why should the medical vision of reality exclude the thoughts and feelings of the patients?

(p. 824)

Why do doctors exclude subjective data?

What reasons can you suggest for omitting subjective data? (You might also think about the fact that some traditions in psychology have taken the view that subjective reports are not legitimate data and should be excluded from laboratory write-ups.)

Donnelly suggests three reasons why doctors do not record subjective information.

1 It is simply not part of the medical tradition to ask patients much about their subjective experience. This level of analysis is not seen as relevant to the practice of medicine.

2 Knowing what symptoms patients experience is increasingly unnecessary for accurate diagnosis. Laboratory tests and use of scanning equipment, rather than the patient's history, is used to reach a definitive diagnosis.

3 It is commonly believed that objective happenings are more real than thoughts and feelings.

Donnelly takes issue with such views, arguing that there are aspects of reality that cannot be encompassed by a purely scientific mode of thinking (for instance, what it is like for a particular person to be sick or disabled?) Donnelly makes the point that stories traditionally construct two landscapes: one of actions or events and one of consciousness. What medicine tends to omit is the consciousness of the person in the story.

Do you think that health care would be improved if doctors and other healthcare professionals were trained to construct medical histories that resembled stories rather than chronicles?

Donnelly argues quite persuasively that if the medical record were to include not only objective facts but also the feelings and ideas of the patients, this would help to humanize the practice of medicine by facilitating empathy in all care givers who hear or read the history. It would also signal to the patient, and others, the doctor's serious interest in patients as people. Healthcare professionals need to ask patients 'What is it like for you?'. Donnelly suggests that it is likely that patients will convey their experiences, their hidden realities, using metaphors.

> Metaphor is in fact no stranger to medicine. Metaphor is an indispensable device to convey the character of pain. We speak of pain as burning, stabbing, knifelike, vicelike, crushing, and the like, using words from the familiar world of sense experience to describe internal distress. We speak of 'burnt out' polycythemia vera and 'smouldering' acute leukaemia. But metaphor is uniquely suited to the task of making tangible the intangible activities of the mind.
>
> *(p. 825)*

1.6 Personal accounts of health

So far in the Trigger Unit we have considered why it is important both for social psychologists and for clinicians to listen to the way individuals experience illness and we have looked at several accounts of illness.

What has been omitted so far, however, is any reference to how different social psychologists might interpret these accounts. In this section we consider how different social psychological perspectives lead to different understandings of what individuals say about their health. In preparation for this section we would like you to review your own state of health.

ACTIVITY 1.6   Simulated survey

Imagine you have been asked to take part in a survey. The interviewer asks you to talk about your health.

Quickly write down a few points which you would be likely to mention about yourself if you were asked about your health. You should prepare your notes or list before you proceed with the rest of this section.

In the next activity you are asked to read nine extracts (located at the end of the unit) in which various public figures provide accounts of their health. This activity will take about 45 — 60 minutes to complete. The purpose is to get you to think about how you interpret the way in which people talk about their health. After reading each extract you should write brief answers to the questions listed below.

You will notice that there is a certain pattern to the accounts because the interviewer (Graham Bridgstock of the *London Evening Standard*) has used some standard questions. At the same time, you will observe differences in what the individuals stress about their health.

After you have read these accounts and formed your own impressions, we will then consider how the perspectives presented in Book 1 might interpret these accounts.

BOX 1.1   A note on Book 1 perspectives

In Book 1 you will be introduced to five theoretical perspectives, all of which have something to say about the person in a social world. The names of these perspectives will give you an idea how they differ in terms of focus:

- the embodied self
- the interpreting self
- the reflexive self
- the distributed self
- the defensive self.

Obviously, at this stage of the course, these phrases will not mean a great deal, but you do not need to be familiar these perspectives to carry out the activity.

Points to note in the accounts

The purpose of this activity is to get you to start thinking about how to interpret personal experience.

Read the accounts and, as you read, make notes on the following features.

- The *key words or themes* in each account.

- The types of explanations of health/illness generated by each of the speakers. Try to broadly categorize the underlying assumptions: e.g. do they strike you as psychological, sociological, biological or cultural? What are the clues that suggest the person is making psychological assumptions or using psychological concepts?

- Any factors which seem to have a bearing on the type of account individuals give to the interviewer.

1.7   Using the Book 1 perspectives to 'read' these accounts

What we will now do is relate the material in these accounts to the perspectives which feature in Book 1. The thesis of this first book is that there are a number of quite distinct ways of thinking about individuals, namely:

- as biological beings (the embodied self)

- as beings who consciously seek to interpret and make sense of our experience (the interpreting self)

- as experiencing, reflexive beings (the reflexive self)

- as beings who are carriers of culture, of social values (the distributed self)

- as beings who are motivated by the conflicts and traumas of childhood (the defensive self).

As we consider how each of these perspectives might be employed to study individual accounts of health and illness, you will be asked to return to your notes to see whether you identified any elements of these perspectives. You should also have available the notes you made for the simulated survey exercise in Activity 1.6 (the points you would have included if you were asked questions about your health) to see how your responses map onto the perspectives.

The embodied self

It is very hard to talk about health without making some reference to the body. Indeed, the questions posed by the interviewer in the *Me and My*

Health series required the respondents to situate their reflections in the context of their bodies e.g. their birth-weight, their present weight, their general body type, their eyesight, episodes of illness or accidents. But at the same time, some accounts seem much more rooted in the body than others. Women's accounts dwell on fertility, pregnancy and childbirth as crucial life experiences. And in view of the emphasis of recent health promotion campaigns, many of the people interviewed show awareness of what counts as a *healthy* life-style. The importance of exercise, diet, moderation in drinking and abstinence from nicotine are frequently noted. (Of course, not all the respondents live by these rules and there is general debate as to the scientific basis of some of the advice.) It struck me how frequently individuals spoke about health as something inherited from their parents. Finally, comments about ageing and death — especially of parents — serve to reminds us of the fragility of the human body. Clearly then, all accounts of health and illness make reference to the person as a biological entity. Birth, death, ageing and accidents all remind us of the fact that we inhabit a body which is a biological system. If we fall, we are likely to break a limb; if we smoke we run the risk of lung cancer. But *none* of the accounts are exclusively concerned with biological events. Valuable as a biological perspective is, we need other vantage points from which to fully understand these accounts and to make sense of health and illness.

> In your notes about yourself did you make references to things about your body: e.g. your height, your weight, your eyesight?

The interpreting self

A second perspective introduced in Book 1 focuses on the cognitive processes we employ to make sense of our social worlds. To what do people attribute their good health (or poor health)? Is health seen as a matter of luck, heredity or a healthy life-style (something you work for and deserve)?

> In an account of your own health, which factors would you be likely to stress?

As you will see when you read Chapter 3 in Book 1 by Mansur Lalljee which presents a cognitive perspective, it has generated much experimental work to test various hypotheses. Researchers have done some interesting work about the way in which we develop and use concepts (or prototypes) such as heart disease or AIDS. A related avenue of investigation looks at how we make sense of our internal states.

Looking at the notes that you made while reading the accounts, did you come across different ways of explaining health or illness? I noted that concepts of luck or good fortune were used by some interviewees: 'I'm naturally optimistic. I tend to wake up every morning thinking: "Hooray, a new day!"' (Claire Tomalin); 'I'm lucky. I can eat anything.' (Max Bygraves). Heredity and family background were cited in a number of the interviews as explanations for mental and physical well-being or its absence. For instance, Virginia Ironside, in explaining her depression, says: 'Whether it's because I was brought up by an alcoholic mother who was depressed or whether it's a genetic thing I don't know. A bit of both, I should think.' Max Bygraves appears to credit his success and good health to the poverty of his early life. He attributes his stamina and health more to good luck than to self discipline.

Another central concern of social psychologists who are interested in how we interpret our experience is the extent to which individuals feel that they have control over events in their lives. Concepts relating to control (e.g. focus of control, learned helplessness) feature in several of these accounts. Reflecting on her father's response to a diagnosis of leukaemia, Virginia Ironside believes that he willed himself to die: '... being sensible, he turned his head to the wall on the Sunday night and didn't wake up, which I think was absolutely right.'

Some of the respondents seek to exercise control over their health by adhering to healthy life-styles e.g. vegetarianism or regular exercise. Believing that mental and physical health are absolutely entwined, Jeff Banks deems himself fortunate in that his religion (Buddhism) has sustained him during difficult periods in his life.

Talking about growing old, Peregrine Worsthorne gives the impression of someone very much in control of his life: 'Everything is still in working order, though I suppose less active than in the prime of life. But then I have never been very physical ... So declining powers don't constitute a tremendous source of misery.'

Jim Davidson, by contrast, describes himself as 'a constant worrier, a terrible panicker, convinced everything is going to go wrong.' He has relied on alcohol to deal with his stress.

The reflexive self

The third perspective you will meet in Book 1 derives from existentialism, humanism and phenomenology, and focuses on subjective experience (in particular from the standpoint of the experiencing person). Richard Stevens, the editor of Book 1 and the author of Chapter 4 on the reflexive self, takes the view that if we are studying the person in a social world, the most significant information is what people are feeling and experiencing. The only way to obtain this knowledge is to introspect on our own experience or ask other people questions or get them to give us accounts of their experience. The task of the social psychologist then becomes that of constructing some understanding of the way in which people make sense of their world.

Does this way of approaching psychology help us to 'read' these accounts that individuals give of their health? To answer this question, you will need to be acquainted with three key existential concerns. These are time, choice and meaningfulness. These dimensions are thought to be relevant to any attempt to understand personal being and social life.

> Look again at your summing up of the different accounts. Did you highlight time, choice or meaningfulness as dominant themes in some or all of the pieces you read?

When I first read through my entire collection of these interviews (nearly 30 in all) I was struck by the fact that most of the accounts were told in such a way that drew attention to the passage of time. Although the information and reflections are not given in a strict chronological order, nonetheless the reader has a sense of time present, time past and time future in all the narratives. Some of the events which are narrated (having to do with birth and early childhood) are clearly not personal memories, but have been passed on to the speaker by their mother or father. 'So she insisted on having me at home in St Peter's Square, Chiswick; she was just lying down after lunch, gave one heave and out I came.' (Claire Tomalin); 'Born at home, sure ... No complications. It was like shelling peas. And I emerged to the strains of Debussy's *Claire de Lune*.' (Jim Davidson).

The theme of time comes out as well when the narrators talk about how they feel about ageing or children growing up or parents dying: 'At 50, I feel a mixture of 65 and eight'; 'The doctor and I are the same age and I realize with horror that she will retire just when I need her'; 'The great thing about being 40 is you've more or less come to terms with yourself.' The existentialists' preoccupation with time then is clearly mirrored in the narratives these individuals construct of their lives.

Similarly, the theme of choice permeates these accounts. Can you recall some of the choices which the narrators included in their stories? Thinking about health and illness, the important choices are to do with life-styles: whether or not to smoke or drink; whether to diet or abstain from fatty, calorie-rich foods; whether to exercise; whether to consult a doctor; whether to take medications; whether to have children. Lynda La Plante gave an example of how she exercised choice by refusing to sign a form to permit an operation on her breast: '... they wanted me to sign to say if they found anything malignant they could operate immediately. But I said: "No, I won't sign." And this woman said: "What d'you mean, you won't sign? ... I've never had anyone not sign before."'

And lastly, the issue of meaning (in the sense of a feeling of engagement or involvement with living) surfaces in quite a few of the accounts. Lynda La Plante's passion for work, even when it threatens her health, comes across strongly: 'I know it's stupid to push myself to exhaustion the way I do. The trouble is I don't notice it until it's too late. Nothing ever stops me. Like yesterday. I got up at 6.30 and had breakfast ... Then I started work and didn't stop till 10 p.m.'

In the same vein, Max Bygraves sees work as a central part of his life: 'Of course I don't need to work now. But then entertaining people, making them laugh, is my life. You can only read so much, play so much golf and sleep so much.'

The way in which children give meaning to life is another theme in several accounts: 'Having children was the best thing that ever happened to me, my salvation. At last life made sense. Almost overnight I could see there was something more important than I was, and that's when I learned to count my blessings, to be happy.' (Maeve Haran); '... when I was bringing him up it put the depression on hold for a while.' (Virginia Ironside).

All the persons interviewed by Graham Bridgstock seem to have a strong sense of purpose. But then perhaps this is to be expected given that he is interviewing individuals who are currently successful in their careers.

Were the themes of time, choice or meaningfulness represented in your notes about your own health?

The distributed self

It may have struck you that none of the perspectives elaborated so far have been primarily concerned with social influences on health. I would imagine, however, that when you read the accounts you identified ways in which social and cultural influences may have shaped the different accounts. The fourth perspective presented in Book 1 is a social constructionist one which argues that the person is *socially constructed*.

Did you find examples to suggest that social variables shape the way that individuals think about their health? Look through your notes to see how many of the accounts seem to hint at the importance of factors such as social class, gender or ethnicity. In some accounts, the impact of class seems quite explicit. For example, Peregrine Worsthorne's story about his mother knowing Dr. Gurevitch, who specialized in injections to make children grow, reminds us that people in different parts of the class structure have differential access to resources. Worsthorne's account is peppered with class allusions. For example he slips in a reference to his father bringing him a Fortnum and Mason hamper with grouse when he was in hospital with jaundice and even a shoulder injury provides the chance to tell us that he was a platoon commander. Max Bygraves, by contrast, paints a picture of working class life and attitudes. He mentions the shared Friday night bath in the iron tub and the home remedies to prevent illness: 'Before bed we'd each have a dose of castor oil with half an orange to take away the taste.'

Diane Abbott's account of having her tonsils out: 'in those days they were whipped out automatically' reminds us of the way in which cultural assumptions can shape medical practice. And her mother's determination to conceal the fact that she had cancer because she felt it had some kind of stigma, is a poignant reminder that the meanings attached to illnesses are socially constructed.

Social constructionism does not restrict the social context to class, gender and ethnicity. The analysis extends to more subtle factors such as the way in which meanings and practices affect what it means to be a person. There are a number of examples which suggest the way in which parental attitudes towards health and illness have a long-term influence on their children. For instance, Diane Abbott tells us that, as a nurse, her mother brought her children up with a robust attitude to health: 'we were never allowed to stay home from school with just a sniff. ... I understand now and just work on regardless.' As the daughter of a Christian Scientist mother, Claire Tomalin was also brought up to believe that 'one was never ill. Mother made light of all ailments.'

Likewise, cultural norms colour how we feel about taking medicine, what we expect from doctors and whether we trust them. Here are a few examples: 'I grew up entirely without medicines; I never had aspirins and I'm still reluctant to take one.' (Claire Tomalin); 'I don't take antibiotics or aspirins' (Diane Abbott).

Another aspect of the socially constructed self is revealed in Lynda La Plante's attitude towards growing old: ' ... I fully intend to have everything lifted, the whole lot done, eyes, lips. I have lines at the top of my lips and I would like those whipped off for a start.'

Much research has been done on gender and health. Did you find evidence of male–female differences when you read these accounts? Although one could point to some obvious gender-related themes (having to do with reproduction and biological differences) I felt that there was much overlap in central themes. This could, however, reflect the sample of individuals chosen and the nature of the questions posed.

The defensive self

We have so far examined four of the five perspectives found in Book 1. It now remains to see what a psychodynamic perspective might contribute to understanding personal accounts of health and illness. Kerry Thomas has written three chapters on the psychodynamic perspective, the first of which appears as Chapter 6 in Book 1. It is quite likely that many of you will have encountered this perspective in previous OU courses. As you may recall, at the heart of the psychodynamic perspective is the view that the structure and the content of the self is constructed during the vital years of babyhood and childhood through interactions with primary carers.

Quickly scan through your notes to see whether you spotted any points in the individual narratives when the speaker mentions the formative influence of early years. Did you note any instances when the person borrowed psychodynamic concepts or dwelt on the relationship between mental health, or psychological wellbeing, and physical health? Try to recall whether in any of the accounts you read the person sought some form of therapy to deal with their problems.

One account which would be amenable to a psychodynamic way of explaining events is that by Virginia Ironside, a well-known agony aunt. Her mother was an alcoholic who tried to commit suicide twice and who left home when her daughter was 14. Virginia's description of her mother portrays her as someone who, at the time of her death, was depressed, living on tranquillisers and biscuits. After her father died, Virginia experienced a recurrence of depression: 'Mine is classic depression. You feel better in the evening, though even then it's as if you're somehow detached, as if there was a pane of glass between you and the rest of the world.'

She goes on to describe how she has tried different cures over the years: pills, 'shrinks', counsellors, group therapy. And the irony of the fact that she spends her life giving advice to others is not lost on Ironside: 'But in fact, being depressed makes you ideally qualified because you spend your entire life trying to find out the answers and on the way acquire a great deal of wisdom, and, while wisdom doesn't necessarily make you happy, it does mean you become quite an expert on the subject. So I don't feel a fraud.'

Virginia Ironside has little doubt that the source of her inner pain stems from her childhood, although she's prepared to admit that there might also be a genetic dimension. In addition, she touches on the issue of separation and loss, a topic which has been of interest to many psycho-dynamic writers and therapists. Ironside suggests that the anxiety she suffers about people going away may be linked to being cared for by au pairs, both of whom left and were never seen again.

The writer Claire Tomalin talks quite openly about going to see a coun-sellor (on the advice of her mother-in-law) because she was having mar-riage problems: 'At first I was resistant to the idea, though I went to see a woman the Tavistock Centre sent me to and never regretted it ... It was more like mother and daughter, and she helped me stick up for myself.'

Therapy also helped Maeve Haran deal with her problems: 'I had ther-apy myself for years, saw a man three time a week. The problem: I would call it lack of confidence, poor self-image. I did very well at school, but lost my nerve at university. It was a fear of being found out, that I wasn't as good as I wanted to be and other people thought I was.'

Curiously enough, reflecting on her experience, Haran is inclined to attribute her problems to heredity: 'You know, melancholia. I just took a long time to build up confidence in myself.' But she felt that she ben-efited from therapy in that it allowed her to experience life instead of being scared of it. Harkening back to her father, she says: 'For years my father was frightened of death and never really enjoyed life.'

ACTIVITY 1.8

Review your notes on your own health

Having read these accounts and having had a preview as to how the perspectives presented in Book 1 might interpret different features of these account, you should now return to the notes you made on your own health for the simulated survey in Activity 1.6 and any additional points you made as you read through the last section.

Do the items on your list show any correspondence to the points emphasized by the different respondents?

Do you feel that the perspectives outlined here provide a useful way of making sense of your experience?

Review of Section 1

This completes our preview of the perspectives found in Book 1. The activities have illustrated the way different perspectives on the person are likely to focus on different aspects of health and illness. The sorts of questions posed and the type of research carried out is very much influenced by the psychologist's initial frame of reference (or perspective). This analysis should prompt you to start thinking about the status of these perspectives and the way in which they relate to one another. Did you find yourself more drawn to certain ways of looking at personhood? If so, why do you think that you are predisposed towards some perspectives or repelled by others? Alternatively, it is possible that you did not view the perspectives as competing for your attention or loyalty. Perhaps you feel inclined to borrow from different perspectives or to seek ways of integrating them.

Don't worry if you are unsure at this stage as to how you would respond to such questions about these different perspectives or the criteria by which you are meant to assess them. The Trigger Unit is not meant to provide an in-depth, technical discussion of these different ways of understanding what it means to be a person. Here our aim is to get you started — you will have the whole course to define your position, to sharpen your understanding and to hear the claims made by representatives of the different perspectives. These same perspectives will feature in Books 2 and 3 of the course, albeit they will be applied to different domains: to social interactions and personal relationships (Book 2) and groups and collectivities (Book 3). And finally, Book 4 will provide you with further opportunities to reflect upon these perspectives and the type of knowledge or understanding they seek to provide.

2 Personal relationships and social interactions in the context of illness

Introduction

Having explored the way in which social psychological perspectives may be applied to the domain of personal experiences of health and illness, we will now turn our attention to the domain of Book 2 — the study of social interaction and personal relations. This book looks at a wide range of personal relationships, including couples, friends and kin, from a variety of perspectives. Here, in the Trigger Unit, we are going to restrict our analysis to relationships which arise in the context of health and illness — *caring relationships*.[1] A central concern will be the different methods that have been used to study topics in this domain. Just as the perspectives introduced in the previous section have relevance outside the domain of personal experience, so, too, the methods outlined in this section have applicability to the other two domains.

Caring relationships

The concept of 'care-taking' and 'care-giving' may seem a bit formal or abstract. Before we proceed to relate this to your personal experience and to a variety of research traditions, spend a few minutes thinking about some of the relationships which might be encompassed by the label 'caring'.

Feedback is given in the 'Feedback for Activities' section on page 101 of this unit.

ACTIVITY 2.1

Caring relationships, for the purposes of this section, are understood as those which exist between:

- a person and his or her care providers (e.g. friends, family, neighbours)
- a person and healthcare professionals.

We will be seeking to understand two issues.

1   What *goes on* in interactions between people under these circumstances, that is, how they communicate with each other.

2   What *lies behind* the observed behaviour, that is, how the participants feel about one another and their respective roles; the social expectations which govern such relationships; what the participants are seeking to achieve — the different agendas of the two parties.

---

[1]Another important set of issues (not covered here but a central topic for health psychology) concerns the way in which personal relationships can have a negative impact on an individual's health. Much has been written about the way in which stress in interpersonal life can lead to ill health.

Nearly all human beings at some stage in their life have the experience of receiving or giving care to another person. For a start, we have all been cared for during infancy and childhood. In addition, we will have all had some encounter, some episode of care, involving healthcare professionals. And many of us have had the experience of providing care to other people — both in professional relationships or in a private, personal capacity. In our analysis we will be restricting our focus to caring relationships where the person who is receiving care is sick or incapacitated.

There is a large literature and research tradition dealing with the relationship between patients and healthcare professionals. Interest in relationships of care which do *not* involve professionals, however, is much more recent. Yet despite this imbalance, most caring is still provided informally, outside the NHS; most caring is carried out by family members, is unpaid and is done by women. If we think about it, this neglect of the informal arrangements for providing care is a rather curious fact. Given the extensive amount of care-giving which is done informally, rather than by paid professionals, one might have supposed that social theorists and researchers would have started from these relationships rather than focusing on relationships with healthcare professionals.

ACTIVITY 2.2

The construction of research topics

Why do you suppose that unpaid, informal caring was not a topic which attracted researchers? Can you suggest four or five reasons for the recent development of literature on this topic?

Feedback is given in the 'Feedback for Activities' section on page 102 of this unit.

2.1   Who are healthcare professionals?

ACTIVITY 2.3

What's in a name?

Who are and who are not healthcare professionals?

Draw up a list of the various groups which you would include under the heading of healthcare professionals.

Now think about the phrase *clinician*. Which professions or professional groups would you label as clinicians?

Community-based healthcare professionals often visit people in their own homes. Their ways of relating to clients are different from hospital-based staff who do not have the same opportunities for long-term relationships

The term *healthcare professionals* is generally understood to include doctors, nurses, physiotherapists, occupational therapists, speech therapists, and dentists. These occupational groups are also commonly referred to as clinicians (i.e. persons with clinical skills). There is lack of agreement as to whether various other groups should be included under the clinician heading. In particular, there is debate as to whether social workers, counsellors, and therapists are clinicians and whether they should be part of the clinical team. (If you want to acquaint yourself with the case for *not* incorporating counselling into the NHS see Harris, 1994.) With the rise of alternative medicine and complementary medicine, we have seen further challenges to who is qualified to diagnose and treat patients. Increasingly, NHS clinicians have been prepared to recommend 'alternative' treatments to their patients. However, it remains to be seen whether the term 'clinician' will be extended to cover some of these additional groups.

2.2 Problematizing the issues

In section 2.5 we will sample some of the literature which focuses on social psychological problems and issues surrounding relationships of care. But since the main purpose of the Trigger Unit is to stimulate you to identify issues and construct problems using your own experience, we will begin this section by asking you to engage in some *problem-based learning*.

You will be asked to identify some key problems which interest you and which you feel are worth investigating and to consider ways of translating your problems into research proposals. We will start this process by focusing attention on interactions with healthcare professionals.

Our first task will be to consider *what* it is that you, as a student of social psychology, want to know about interactions between people and healthcare professionals. Second, you will be asked to generate ideas as to how we could study these interactions. After you have developed your own *research agenda* you will be asked to review samples of typical work in this area.

This approach should:

- allow you to practise your general skills as social psychological observers and theorists

- stimulate you to think about methodological issues e.g. how to collect data

- develop your competence in reading social psychological research

- provide you with an opportunity to compare your thinking on the topic with that of professionals in the field.

Justifying your research

As well as gaining experience in formulating research problems, the would-be social psychologist must learn to defend or justify his or her research proposals. As an undergraduate student, this may be just a matter of explaining to your tutor why you think it important or useful to do a research project or dissertation on your chosen topic. As a postgraduate student you will need to convince members of a research degree committee that your proposal is 'do-able' and 'worthwhile'. As a professional researcher seeking research funding, you will need to put your case to a bigger and perhaps more specialist audience.

To a large measure, what you are doing when you justify your work is to anticipate how your findings will fit into a bigger picture. The picture you select as your reference point will vary depending on the type of research you propose carrying out. In some cases your background orientation may be a theoretical landscape; in other cases your backdrop may be the world of policy and decision making.

What questions should you pose?

For someone new to a discipline, one of the most important skills to acquire is that of identifying suitable problems, of learning how to pose questions. In the activity that follows, you will be asked to spend some time formulating questions about the social interactions which take place between patients and healthcare professionals.

The art of identifying important issues ACTIVITY 2.4

Ideally, you should try to do the entire activity before you read the rest of the section and you should try to do it at one go, but if this proves difficult, try to do the first two parts together.

You should allow yourself about 40 minutes in which to carry out the complete activity.

The purpose of this activity on question formulation is to encourage you to reflect on the way in which you go about organizing your knowledge and your thoughts when approaching a new topic. (Remember to refer to your Resource File.)

1 Prepare a list of 3—4 key questions you want to ask about social interactions between patients and healthcare professionals. (You should not at this stage be worried about the existing literature. If you feel you are at a loss as to where to start, I suggest you scan a newspaper or a magazine to pick up ideas. For example, suppose you came across an article about euthanasia, what issues might this suggest?)

2 For each question, jot down a few reasons *why* you want to ask this question? (Why is it significant? What would you expect to find or to prove?)

3 Spend a few minutes reflecting on your hunches and your beliefs about relationships between patients and healthcare professionals.

4 Think about the possible origins of your beliefs. Do they derive from first-hand experience or from the experience of those close to you or from what you hear from others, or from what you read in newspapers or see on television?

5 Do your beliefs derive from or reflect a particular world view? (Is there a theoretical or ideological underpinning?) Do you think that you have any preconceptions concerning healthcare professionals?

2.3 Choosing a research method

At this point you should have prepared a list of questions you think are worth asking. Select one or two of these questions and think about the sorts of methods you could use to investigate your problems. Thinking back to the sorts of research methods you have learned about in other courses, try to generate a checklist of all the ways in which you might study social interactions between patients and healthcare professionals. Then take this a step further and complete Activity 2.5 on the strengths and limitations of the different methods.

ACTIVITY 2.5   To organize your thoughts, fill in the table given below. Don't worry about completing all the boxes. Spend about 15 minutes on the activity before you read on.

Table 1   Methods for studying interactions with healthcare professionals

Method	Strengths	Limitations

Table 1   (continued)

Method	Strengths	Limitations

Research methods

Here is a synopsis of some of the different methods which you might select to research interactions and relationships between patients and healthcare professionals. Compare this to your own list.

1   Direct observation

The researcher goes out into the field (e.g. to an out-patient clinic or a GP surgery) and looks at what happens. The researcher may sit to one side and take notes, use a video or one-way screen, or tape the interaction. Participant observation is a special form of observation where the observer has a role in the world he or she is observing. Although this method may sound easy in theory, when it comes to practice, observational research requires much preparation and entails many pitfalls. (You will discover this for yourself when you do the first project which is designed to get you to try out the method. Also, the first television programme will deal with the problem of how we observe and how we make sense of what we have observed.)

Strengths: The data collected at a consultation is immediate and first hand because it is collected as the interview, consultation or episode of care unfolds. A trained outside observer should be impartial and able to step back from what is going on. The researcher can simultaneously observe both the patient and the professional (as well as the setting). If you tape or video the encounter, you can go back over it at a later time, show it to others, look for subtle or missed cues (i.e. carry out what is called microanalysis). Examples of direct observation work undertaken by researchers will be described later in this section of the Trigger Unit.

Limitations: There may be problems gaining access to the clinical consultation (e.g. ethical problems, patient consent). It may be hard or impossible to obtain a representative sample of patients and healthcare professionals to take part in the study. There is the impact of the observer on the interaction to consider: it is not always easy to collect data in a non-intrusive manner and there is always the question of how much the presence of the observer influences the interaction. Finally, it is not so easy in the field situation to remain neutral or impartial.

2   Retrospective interviews

The researcher may decide to talk to patients or professionals *after* the interaction has occurred. For example, mothers taking their babies for a routine visit could be interviewed after their appointment with the nurse or doctor. Here the data is the participants' account of what has occurred.

Strengths: Such interviews are likely to be easier to arrange than direct observations of interactions. Retrospective studies avoid the problem of possible observer influences on the interaction. It is probably easier to obtain a large number of interviews (compared with direct observation).

Limitations: You may only be able to sample the views of one set of participants (either patients or healthcare professionals). It is not easy to cross-check the accuracy or reliability of what the respondents tell you.

3   Group discussions

The researcher may bring together a group of patients and professionals or a group of patients or a group of clinicians or members of self-help groups to discuss experiences of consultations or ongoing caring relationships. The data in this type of research could either be spontaneous accounts or responses to open-ended questions. For example, a researcher working with a carers' association might organize a meeting of people caring for elderly parents to hear about their experiences in trying to arrange respite care.

Strengths: This is an efficient way to sample a wide range of attitudes and experiences. Some people may feel more relaxed if interviewed in a group rather than in a one-to-one situation. In the discussion, the ideas or comments of one individual may spark off hidden or buried views in other contributors.

Limitations: In a group situation, participants may agree with attitudes or voice opinions which are at variance with what they would say if they were on their own or what they 'really' believe. Individuals may 'go along with the group' or they may exaggerate or distort comments in order to win attention or approval. In other words, there are many uncontrolled group dynamic factors at work in such interviews. At the same time, one could argue that in a group situation individuals are more liberated, more willing to voice subversive or anti-social or nonconformist views.

4   *Analysis of various documents*

Using methods such as content analysis or structural analysis, the researcher may review written material or other media (such as films, radio or television programmes) with a view to identifying key issues, themes, types of discourse, ideologies or recurrent images. The written documents could include reports, journal articles, training documents, syllabuses, novels, or short stories. One study has looked at the type of advice given to mothers by studying child care manuals written by healthcare professionals (Wolfenstein, 1951). The documents you collect for your Resource File could provide the raw material for this method.

Strengths: This method allows a researcher to explore the broader social context within which patients' and professionals' interpersonal relations are situated. It also makes it possible to investigate changes over time and cross-cultural differences. For example, one could look at information leaflets produced in the 1940s and compare them with materials produced today to see what these suggest about the 'good' patient or the power relationship between patients and doctors.

Limitations: Because it appears to be a less technical method, there is a danger that researchers who use document analysis may not receive proper training. As a consequence, they may fail to plan their work properly (e.g. the sampling of documents) and the results may be criticized for lacking rigour and objectivity. More importantly, there is a lack of agreement as to how to 'read' or interpret documents, film or radio material. Some methods of content analysis attempt to be rigorous and quantitative, but others are far more qualitative (and, some would say, *subjective* and not replicable).

5   Case studies of complaints and litigation

The researcher may decide to interview lawyers or bodies which represent dissatisfied patients, or groups such as the Medical Defence Union
which represent doctors who are threatened with legal action. This could
be combined with a study of relevant documents. Newspapers quite
often carry articles dealing with alleged malpractice. (Have you come
across such material when scanning the papers for items for your
Resource File?)

Strengths: Although I have not identified research by social psychologists
which employs this method, it strikes me as a suitable way of looking at
issues concerning mis-communication and the breakdown of relations
between professionals and patients. Examining what happens under
these conditions may provide insights into more normal relations. When
do patients sue healthcare professionals? Is there a pattern to the types of
complaints patients bring against doctors? Have these changed over a
period of 40—50 years?

Limitations: By their very nature, such accounts are likely to be emotionally charged. Legal documents may not necessarily tell us very much
about day-to-day interactions and communications. Indeed, they may
produce a very biased way of looking at relationships. There could be
problems in gaining access to such materials. And finally, there is the
whole issue of which patients have access to lawyers.

6   Experimental study

The essence of the experimental method is to have one or more groups
who receive one type of 'treatment' and a control group who do not
receive the experimental treatment or who receive a 'standard' treatment. For instance, a researcher interested in health promotion might
select one group of patients to receive advice about giving up smoking
from practice nurses who have attended training session, a second group
who are given a leaflet and a third, control, group to whom no advice is
offered.

Strengths: The experimental method is thought by many to be the best
way to test hypotheses. Ideally, the researcher randomly assigns subjects
to groups and carries out pre- and post-test measures. The logic of the
method is that by eliminating or controlling all extraneous factors, the
experimenter will be able to attribute any differences between the groups
to the independent variable. This method seeks to demonstrate causal
relationships between variables, rather than covariation.

Limitations: It has not proved easy to apply the experimental method to
the study of social behaviour. For a start, many of the independent variables which interest social psychologists are difficult to operationalize
and hard to measure. This is because, firstly, many of the phenomena
which interest psychologists are very complex, making it hard to
manipulate them in a meaningful way. (How would you vary self-esteem
in an experiment?) Secondly, there are ethical problems relating to the

treatment of human subjects, for example, is it permissible to deceive subjects or to expose them to painful or embarrassing situations? Finally, there has been much debate about the validity of experimental studies. Some critics feel that it is difficult to generalize from the contrived environment of the laboratory to everyday social situations.

Quite often researchers combine methods, leading to more complex research designs. For example, the researcher could observe an interaction, interview the participants afterwards *and* study written documents pertaining to the interaction (e.g. notes written by the doctor or nurse). The first television programme which deals with methods of observation shows how methods can be combined: you will observe a surgeon talking to a patient and you will hear from the participants what they were hoping to achieve in the interview.

> How does this list of methods compare with yours? Have we missed out any methods which are on your list? Were there any methods which had not occurred to you?

In connection with these research methods, a variety of different measuring instruments can be used to collect and structure the data such as questionnaires, interview schedules, attitude scales or observational rating scales. Your D317 projects will introduce you to a variety of methods of data collection, such as content analysis, using a coding frame and the use of rating scales.

Further reading

An eclectic set of papers by Daly et al. (1992) includes a section on qualitative methods. This would be a useful starting point for anyone wanting help in developing a research proposal. You may also wish to look at Banister et al. (1994), your methods book which covers all the qualitative methods that you will need for your projects.

Difficulties of generalizing

As a student of social psychology, one issue that you will meet again and again will be how far you can generalize from a single study. No matter how well constructed the research, there are always limitations which derive from elements such as its setting, the time it was done and the culture within which it was carried out.

Indeed, one of the factors which distinguishes social science findings from evidence produced in the natural sciences is that the meaning or interpretation of the results (and their applicability to other cultures or social settings) cannot be taken for granted. These comments may be a bit more meaningful if we consider the issue of generalizability in the context of studies of health and illness.

ACTIVITY 2.6   **Generalizing about clinical consultations**

Think about some of the problems that arise in making generalizations about what goes on in clinical consultations. Suppose you designed an observational study of GPs and their patients to determine whether the introduction of computers into the surgery was altering the way in which GPs interact with their patients. What are some of the factors you would need to think about if you wanted to be able to generalize from one practice to others?

A very high proportion of British GPs (more than 60 per cent) now use a computer

How would you sample practices, doctors and patients? Would you be able to generalize from general practice to other specialisms (e.g. obstetrics and gynaecology) or to make statements as to the way in which computers might impinge on other healthcare professionals?

Feedback is given in the 'Feedback for Activities' section on page 103 of this unit.

Another constraint on generalizing is time. In studying social events, 20 or 30 years may bring enormous social changes. Social attitudes may shift, scientific knowledge may alter, behaviour patterns may change; in addition, there may be political upheavals, technological advances, and changes to the economic infrastructure of the society. Just think of the changes that have taken place over the last 30 years in the way in which health care is organized and delivered in the UK. Such changes mean that some research on doctor–patient relations carried out 30 years ago may no longer be relevant. Culture is another factor which needs to be considered when trying to generalize: are the results of research carried out in a suburban health clinic relevant to an urban, multicultural group practice?

Relationships between patients and professionals do not exist in a vacuum. They are conditioned by a whole range of factors at both the individual and the societal level.

Although the sociocultural dimensions of health and illness will be considered in the examples of research given in section 2.5 and will be the focus of the final part of the Trigger Unit, you might at this stage like to reflect on the types of sociocultural variables which shape our relationships with healthcare professionals.

Sociocultural factors shaping public expectations　　　　　　ACTIVITY 2.7

What would you consider to be the three or four most significant factors shaping public expectations? Is there any reason to believe that expectations have shifted over the last 20 or 30 years?

Feedback is given in the 'Feedback for Activities' section on page 103 of this unit.

2.4　Contact with healthcare professionals

On the whole, interaction with healthcare professionals is initiated by the patient. So, one research issue is 'Why do people decide (or not decide) to consult a doctor when they are ill?'

Decisions about seeing a doctor　　　　　　ACTIVITY 2.8

When was the last time you saw your GP? Can you recall the purpose of the visit? Did you hesitate before you made the appointment? Have you ever requested a health check from your GP?

On the whole, how often do you see a doctor or other healthcare professional: monthly, once a year, once every couple of years?

Can you recall a recent illness when you decided *not* to consult a doctor? If so, what made you decide to deal with the matter yourself? If you have responsibility for an infant or child, how do you decide whether to seek medical advice? (Think about the last time you had to make a decision on behalf of a minor or someone else.)

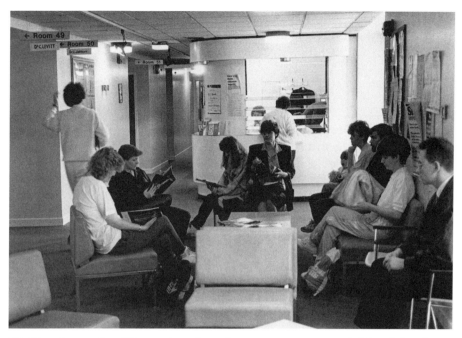

Waiting to see the GP: most patient–doctor encounters are initiated by the patient

Several studies have examined the reasons why some ill people consult a doctor, while others with the same complaint do not.

In many countries these differences may be explained because people cannot afford to pay for medical care. However 'even when they *can* afford it there is often little correlation between the severity of a physical illness and the decision to seek medical help ... studies have shown that abnormal symptoms[2] are common in the population, but only a small percentage are brought to the attention of doctors' (Helman, 1990, p. 114).

What this suggests is that a number of *non*-physiological factors influence the 'pathways to the doctor'. Zola (1973) outlined five such factors:

1   the availability of medical care

2   whether the patient can afford it

3   the failure, or success, of treatments within the popular or folk sectors (e.g. home remedies, preparations available from the chemist without a prescription)

4   how the patient perceives the problem

5   how others around the patient perceive the problem.

---

[2]Abnormal symptoms include tiredness, various aches and pains, lack of energy, inability to sleep, loss of appetite, bowel problems, headaches.

Epidemiological studies (research into the patterns of disease in a population) confirm this discrepancy between the amount of abnormal signs and symptoms found in the population and the number of people who go to see a doctor. Dunnell and Cartwright (1972) report that 91 per cent of their sample of adults had experienced one or more abnormal symptoms in the two weeks preceding the study, but only 16 per cent had consulted a doctor during this time. To make sense of this finding one needs to examine how and when abnormal symptoms lead to the person labelling themselves as ill enough to seek professional help.

2.5   Research into relationships between patients and healthcare professionals

In this section you are presented with examples of research studies which are intended to help you make connections between your own interests and expertise, and the work of professional social researchers who study personal relationships and interactions. We start by looking at healthcare professionals and we conclude by looking at more informal care. We will also relate the research to the different perspectives social psychologists use to study and explain the interpersonal domain. The empirical studies have been selected because they use different methods and represent different theoretical perspectives.

Research Study 1: Relationships between patients and healthcare professionals

This research study is based on *Hard-earned Lives: Accounts of Health and Illness from East London* by Jocelyn Cornwell (1984).

Jocelyn Cornwell, a geographer working in East London, researched commonsense ideas and theories about health, illness and the health service. She provides an analysis of the way in which her respondents talked about their health and their experience with doctors. This research is relevant to the concerns of the Trigger Unit and Book 2 of the course because it illustrates the fact that, in social relationships, participants frequently have more than one interpretation of what is going on. What they tell a researcher may depend on their relationship to the interviewer and their perception of what the researcher is seeking. Consequently, research which adopts a strict 'outsider's' view of relationships may misunderstand or oversimplify their nature. Finally, the research is interesting in that it demonstrates that social research itself is a form of social interaction.

BOX 2.1 Cornwell's research design

Cornwell studied 24 people in East London, using what is called an ethnographic or case study approach which derives from social anthropology. In her work, Cornwell investigated health in relation to other aspects of social life. 'In general, the ethnographic approach is one that encourages attention to the detail of people's lives and thus to the differences between individuals.' (p. 203)

What Cornwell did was to get to know the people in her study individually and to find out about the quality of their relationships. People were recruited through their informal networks. Individuals were interviewed several times and the interviews were tape-recorded. The interviews were constructed around a schedule of topics, and included standard questions and questions tailored for individuals.

ACTIVITY 2.9   **A simulated interview**

This is meant to be a brief activity — part I should take you no more than 5 or 10 minutes to write a few notes; part 2 will take longer — but it's the sort of activity you might be able to fit into a social encounter.

Part 1

Imagine that you are being interviewed by Cornwell about your relationships with doctors and answer the following questions:

What is your image of a 'good' doctor?

How easy do you find talking to your doctor?

Do you have children? If Yes: Did you (or your partner) attend ante-natal clinics when you were pregnant?

If Yes, why?

If No, why not?

Part 2

If feasible, try asking two or three people you know to answer these questions.

When you reflect upon the way you (and any volunteers you were able to question) replied to these questions, you should think about two different issues:

1   the content of the replies: the range of replies people give to such questions; the words or phrases used; the ways of structuring an answer

2   the mental processes which go on when you try to answer such questions; the assumptions you need to make in order to produce a reply; whether you felt that you might construct different responses depending on the circumstances.

If you have taken previous social science courses, you will be aware that answers to interview questions will be influenced by diverse factors, including, for example, whether the interviewer establishes rapport with the person being interviewed, the precise way in which questions are framed and the respondent's understanding of the nature and purpose of the interview. One situational factor which Cornwell draws attention to in her analysis of her findings is the *context* in which the person gives their account.

Ways of eliciting accounts   ACTIVITY 2.10

Do you think that you would give different answers to questions about health and healthcare professionals depending on the way in which the information was collected?

Try to work out how your replies might differ in these circumstances.

1   You are on your own with an interviewer.

2   You are filling in an anonymous questionnaire.

3   You are taking part in a public debate and you are part of a large group.

4   You are with a group of friends swapping stories about doctors and your experience of the health service.

5   You are talking to your doctor.

Would some of your answers be more 'truthful' than others?

From her own work and from studying the findings of other researchers Cornwell found that results obtained from talking to people about healthcare services were complex and often contradictory. The way she made sense of these inconsistencies was to look at the variations between what she called *public* and *private* accounts: 'The public accounts tended to occur in answer to questions which were put to people directly about doctors and health services. The private accounts were usually contained in the narrative of episodes which involved doctors but in which the doctors' activities were not the focus of attention.' (p. 171)

Public accounts of healthcare professionals

When asked direct questions, Cornwell's respondents expressed admiring and respectful attitudes toward doctors and toward medicine generally. Statements such as 'doctors are a breed, a certain breed of person' and 'all doctors are good doctors' were typical of public accounts: 'To me, doctors and even nurses, this [offering respect] is something you do. I do, because to me they're doing a job I could never do and therefore I look up to them. I'm not saying they're all perfect but I still look up to them.' (p. 174)

How would you explain such positive evaluations of doctors in public   ACTIVITY 2.11
accounts?

Public accounts, according to Cornwell are 'sets of meanings in common currency that reproduce and legitimate the assumptions people take for granted about the nature of social reality'.

> There is a public account of most subjects which occur with any regularity in everyday conversations, the point being that in sticking to the public account of whatever it is they are discussing — whether it is work, or money, husbands, mothers, children, or the local doctor — the person doing the talking can be sure that whatever they say will be acceptable to other people.
>
> *(p. 15)*

Cornwell maintains that such attitudes derive from 'the assumption that doctors are highly trained, scientific and technical workers who know things that ordinary people do not know'. Her respondents repeatedly drew attention to the length of time it takes to become a doctor, to the fact that doctors have to study and learn from books and that being a doctor requires qualifications. So public accounts tend to reflect what are assumed to be shared social values.

People had very clear expectations as to what a good doctor should do: enquire about the patient's symptoms, conduct a physical examination, make a diagnosis and prescribe a treatment. In the event that the patient does not improve or the doctor is unable to make a diagnosis, the expectation was that the patient would be referred to a specialist. Adherence to this sequence of steps led to patients being happy with their doctor; deviation from the script led to criticisms. There were age difference as to how respondents viewed healthcare professionals and what they expected of them. Older people had more respect for doctors whom they saw as socially superior beings. They respected professionals for their qualifications. Younger people showed signs of being more critical.

ACTIVITY 2.12

The shaping of public discourse about healthcare professionals

What shapes these public accounts of medicine that we've been looking at? On the one hand, first-hand contact with healthcare professionals is likely to exert a powerful influence on the way individuals come to perceive doctors. Another possible influence is the public images of the professions disseminated by the mass media. We will be looking at such images in the final section of the Trigger Unit, but at this stage you might try to make an inventory of these images.

Over the next few days, make a conscious effort to look for images of healthcare professionals in the mass media, and, where possible, add them (or notes about them) to your Resource File.

Are the images consistent? Do you think that some images are more common than others?

Cornwell maintains that images of medical practice and the medical profession play a powerful role in shaping the way in which her subjects thought about and talked about health matters: ' ... the images dominate the ideological framework within which people make sense of their experience to such an extent that when there is a discrepancy between the two, the experience and not the image is made redundant.' (p. 197)

She suggests that the positive image of the medical profession overrides memories people have of 'bad' doctors, wrong diagnoses, prescriptions that are unwanted and do not work. This tendency for positive images to dominate public accounts comes out when Cornwell compares and contrasts public and private accounts. The public accounts people gave recreated and reproduced images of medicine that bore no relationship to their personal experience.

Private accounts of healthcare professionals

While Cornwell found the content of public accounts to be uniform and predicable, this was *not* true of private accounts generated spontaneously by respondents. Private accounts consisted mostly of stories about how a particular doctor behaved on a particular occasion. In contrast to public accounts, these were idiosyncratic and often contradictory. In addition they were far more critical of the health care offered them and of healthcare professionals.

One recurrent theme in the public accounts was the doctor's power and the social distance this created between doctors and patients. Many interviewees told stories about outwitting doctors, or getting the better of them. What such stories reveal is that the person telling the story felt involved in an unequal contest. Experience of medical power and authority was felt most intensely in hospital settings. (The issue of power and authority will be a central theme in Book 2.)

Judging from the language and subject matter of private accounts, encounters with doctors tend to be emotionally charged events for patients. The emotions doctors aroused in their patients were frequently the product of the patient's subordinate position. Emotional rage against doctors occurs when they fail to live up to the patient's expectations. When things go wrong, the tendency is to hold doctors completely and personally responsible. At one level, there is an expectation that doctors should know everything and not make mistakes. At the same time, what came across in private accounts was that patients stored up in their memory acts of kindness or thoughtfulness.

What do patients want or expect of doctors? Cornwell's data suggest that users of health services make a distinction between what is essential and what would be nice, but not easy to deliver. There is also, at least in public accounts, a tendency to make excuses for doctors. This suggests that patients understand the peculiar, ambiguous nature of patient–doctor relationships. On the one hand the relationship is private and intimate, but at the same time it is essentially a professional relationship. Thus, the patient wants the doctor to go through the motions of being pleasant, sociable and caring, but, at the same time, the patient is aware that she or he is really just a number. You are aware that as the doctor is talking to you, part of his/her mind is calculating how many more patients there are to see before lunch or before it is time to go home and relax.

Reflections on Cornwell's study

When you study Book 2 you will find that Cornwell's research shows some interesting convergences with trends in the study of social interaction. Alan Radley in Chapter 2 argues that an important shift has occurred in the way social psychologists study social relationships. This has entailed a growing recognition of the need for observers to take account of what it is that social actors are seeking to achieve. Ichheiser (an Austrian sociologist) was one the first to propose that how we act depends upon impressions that others might form of us. In turn we modify our behaviour to foster an impression that we wish others to form. If we accept this view of interaction, then researchers need to take account of the point of view of the participants. Instead of adopting an 'outside' view, researchers need to be tuned-in to the 'inside' view of the social actors themselves.

In the context of Cornwell's research, the idea that the interviewees were trying to *perform* for the researcher could help us to make sense of apparent discrepancies in the explanations of health and illness given by her respondents. When she was just getting to know her respondents and when she was conducting formal interviews, the people she talked to were likely to 'put on a performance' and tell her what they thought she wanted to hear. If this tendency is not realized, the researcher may give undue emphasis to clichés and polite discourses, transforming them into 'what people think' or 'what people believe'. What Cornwell's work reveals is that much of what respondents tell the researcher may be '... the products of a particular kind of social contract in which the interviewee offers the interviewer what they (the interviewee) assume the researchers expects to hear.' (Rogers, 1991, p. 78).

In ethnographic research of this type, as field work proceeds and the researcher becomes more accepted and trusted, the social distance between the researcher and the interviewees is reduced: '[Cornwell] did this by spending a lot of time with them, attending social gatherings and showing herself to be separate from 'them', i.e. the medical establishment — for example, by smoking in interviewees' company.' (p. 79)

Under these circumstances, the interviewees were prepared to offer more private accounts. (Cornwell's distinction between public and private accounts has parallels with the distinction journalists and their interviewees make between 'official' views and what is 'off the record'. But as many politicians have discovered to their dismay, journalists do not always subscribe to these rules and words which slip out after a good meal and a bottle of wine may appear in the public domain.)

The ambivalence people in Cornwell's study expressed about doctors could be explored using a different perspective — the psychodynamic model. Given the expertise and authority of doctors (formally acknowledged by Cornwell's interviewees), they may well have served as father figures, thereby triggering unresolved childhood conflicts. In Chapter 4 of Book 2 Kerry Thomas explores the psychodynamics of relating. Although her chapter deals specifically with patients and analysts, there is a long history of using these ideas to study the relationship between GPs and patients.

Michael Balint (1964), who trained in both medicine and psychoanalysis, sought to translate the insights of psychoanalysis into general practice. He suggests that an important task of the doctor is to get behind what patients say to find out what they 'really' mean. He stresses the type of mutual investment that GPs and patients place in their relationship. Unlike hospital medicine where the patient and consultant may only meet one or two times, in general practice each consultation builds on the previous episode. Consequently, GPs are in a position to use their extensive background knowledge about their patients. This realization led Balint to suggest that the most powerful therapeutic tool the doctor possessed was him or herself. Many patients visit the doctor to get a 'dose of doctor'. In these cases it is the human relationship which has the most effect on patients' welfare (Armstrong, 1989, p. 73).

Research Study 2: Patients and professionals: the nature of the encounters

In our first research study, the researcher sought to find out what people felt about doctors by asking them to comment on this relationship. In this section the focus will shift to research on the nature of the doctor–patient relationship which looks at the interaction itself. Rather than focus on a single study, here we will select from different research to get an insight into the tensions and dynamics of this relationship.

A major challenge facing social psychology is how to reconcile two seemingly incompatible observations about social interactions and personal relationships. On the one hand there is a sense in which all social exchanges appear *unique and unpredictable*. Before an interaction begins, no one can be certain how the participants will behave. At the same time, we also experience a *patterning* to social interaction; we sense that there are regularities which make it possible for us to operate, if we choose, on automatic pilot. And we are also aware of *constraints* (e.g. time, power differentials). Book 2 addresses this paradox regarding interactions which extends to the way in which we experience relationships. Personal relationships are at one and the same time dynamic (changing, continuously being negotiated) *and* predictable. The authors of Book 2 seek to demonstrate that in recent years there has been a gradual shift in the types of questions social psychologists working in this domain ask and the type of research carried out. One way of characterizing this shift is to say that psychologists no longer restrict themselves to an outside view of what is going on between people. Instead there is a recognition that to understand events, we need to have an inside view. We need to understand how the participants themselves view the interaction or the relationship. This often means accepting ambiguities rather than seeing these as errors or inaccuracies in the data collection process. Another important development in the study of interactions and relationships has been a rethinking of the nature of social action so that, instead of using a cause and effect model, researchers are more concerned with trying to find out how understandings develop, how social action unfolds.

A bias in the research

Patients' relationships with *doctors* have been much researched: '... the nature of consultations; patterns of communication, diversity of goals and consequent bargaining during consultation, sources of satisfaction and dissatisfaction with the consultation process, all have received attention.' (Miles, 1991, p. 153)

However, as Miles goes on to point out, there has been much less attention paid to relationships with other healthcare professionals:

> By comparison, similar aspects of patients' relationships with professionals other than doctors have been less studied so that discussion of research findings tends to focus mostly on patients' encounters with doctors. Indeed, doctors, as the most powerful profession in the health labour force, have been able to influence the expectations, the goals and the actions of patients and of other professionals, dominating the consultation process to an extent that these others have not matched, a factor which may explain research bias towards the study of patients' relationships with doctors rather than these other professionals.
>
> (p. 152)

The reason for mentioning this bias in the literature is to make clear why most of the research cited in this section relates to doctors. In reading the material, if you come from a different clinical background, you should ask yourself how and why interactions and professional relationships differ.

The nature of the clinical consultation interview

In our society, most encounters with doctors and other professional groups are formal encounters, taking the form of consultation interviews. Social researchers have tried to identify some of the essential features of this type of social encounter and the ensuing relationship.

ACTIVITY 2.13   **Characterizing the consultation**

Do you think there is anything unique about encounters with healthcare professionals? Is there anything that makes patient–doctor interactions different from other social encounters?

Stimson and Webb (1975) identified three features which characterize consultations.

1 They take place at restricted appointed times and in specific places.

2 There is a specific reason for the interaction.

3 There is a competence gap between the advice seeker and the advice giver.

But while these features characterize doctor–patient encounters, they also apply to a whole range of other social interactions. For example:

- seeing a lawyer

- attending a tennis lesson with a professional coach

- having a piano lesson with a teacher.

Many years ago, Goffman (1961) suggested that what is special about the doctor–patient type of encounter is that it is a focused interaction in which both parties try to sustain a single focus of attention. There is a fairly predictable structure to this type of encounter. As we saw in the last section, Cornwell's interviewees had very clear expectations as to what a good GP should do. Yet despite the fact that there is a general familiarity with the script, patients often feel they are not able to raise issues that concern them. They report being easily put off during the consultation.

Do doctors make you feel ill at ease?   ACTIVITY 2.14

Does this finding coincide with your personal experience? Why do you think that people find the relationship with healthcare professionals so difficult?

Do any of the items in your Resource File support the idea that there are problems surrounding the doctor–patient relationship?

Miles (1991) singles out *expectations* as the critical social psychological factor shaping encounters with healthcare professionals:

> ... the two participants come to the consultation each with a set of expectations as to how they will both behave and each with one or more goals which they want to attain. Actual behaviour during the consultation is influenced by the expectations and goals of the two participants and by the perception of each of the conduct of the other. Whether expectations are shared or different, whether the goals are similar or not, will have a major impact on the consultation.

(p. 153)

This analysis by Miles echoes some of the themes which are developed throughout Book 2. In Chapter 2, Alan Radley compares early research on social interaction (which introduced the concepts of norms and roles as key explanatory ideas) with present-day social psychological ways of thinking about what goes on in social life. By focusing on the repertoires of verbal and non-verbal behaviours available to people, some of the earlier work tended to give the impression that social interaction is largely pre-determined. As you will discover when you study Book 2, many contemporary social psychologists feel that social interaction is much more open and ambiguous than this initial work indicated.

Patterns of communication

One topic that has attracted a large amount of research attention has been communications between patients and professionals. According to Thompson (1984) many patients are dissatisfied with the way in which doctors communicate:

> … dissatisfaction with medical communications remains the most prominent of patient complaints and a major factor in the move to alternative medicine, with its focus on good and reassuring communications and the patient as an informed participant in treatment. Patients prefer to be able to give an account of their problems in their own terms, yet these expectations of communication are often unmet.

> *(p. 87)*

ACTIVITY 2.15   Do your own personal experiences confirm or refute these statements? How would you rate your doctor's communication skills?

Most of the work on communications has been carried out in general practice. An example of a typical study is the work of Byrne and Long (1976) which analysed 2,000 tape-recorded GP consultations. What they found was that over three-quarters of interviews were 'doctor-centred'. What doctors did was to concentrate on closed questions (i.e. questions which lead to 'yes' or 'no' types of answers) about the *first* complaint the patient presented. They brushed aside or ignored verbal leads about other problems. This method of consultation allowed doctors to make a quick organic diagnosis. The other 25 per cent of the GPs were more 'patient-centred'.

ACTIVITY 2.16   **Explaining 'doctor-centred' interviews**

Why do you think doctors behaved in this way? Do you think that this finding is still valid now? Before you read the next section, generate a list of all the possible hypotheses you can think of to explain Byrne and Long's finding.

Possible reasons for doctor-centred interviews

1   The way in which doctors are trained; emphasis on science, neglect of interpersonal skills.

2   The type of people who are attracted to medicine in the first place.

3   A lack of time (an average consultation lasts eight minutes); pressures of work means the doctor takes the lead to speed things up.

4   Doctors are the experts; they know more than patients, hence it makes sense for them to lead the interview.

5   Doctors are afraid of patients; they feel better if they maintain control of the interview.

6   Doctors believe that this is what patients expect of them.

Are these hypotheses mutually exclusive? Is there one which you think is the most important factor? How might you research them?   ACTIVITY 2.17

Efforts to improve communications

Studies on communication patterns raise expectations about improving relationships. Can research evidence about doctor–patient interactions be used to change what goes on in the consulting room? This section suggests ways in which social psychological findings can be applied.

Quite often the solution to these problems is seen in terms of the need to train or educate doctors. Indeed, nearly all healthcare professionals are now receiving some basic training in communication skills, using role play techniques, simulated patients and video recordings. However, what about approaching the problem from the other direction? Do you think there might be any mileage in seeking to train patients so that they are able to take on a more active role when they visit their GP or a consultant?

According to Stimson and Webb, patients are alert to the fact that there is limited time available when they see their doctor and therefore rehearse a brief coherent account which they attempt to provide in the opening few minutes of the interview, *before the doctor takes over the agenda.* Although there is evidence that nearly all patients go to see the doctor with at least one request or question they want to put to the doctor, less than half will spontaneously express it. 'This suggests that, unless carefully encouraged, patients may withhold requirements and then leave the consultation dissatisfied with the advice they have been given.' (p.93)

At the time of writing this unit, the Patient's Charter is seeking to make users of the NHS more aware of their rights as consumers of health services. Whether this produces changes in patient behaviour remains to be seen. Here we point to some attempts that have been made to educate patients.

ACTIVITY 2.18 **Approaches to patient training**

Before you read the next section, you should explore your own preliminary thoughts on the matter. Do you think it is feasible to train patients? Do you think that you personally could benefit from such training?

Have you had any contact with self-help groups or patient groups e.g. an asthma support group or a multiple sclerosis group? Self-help groups and some of the work done by women's health groups could be described as educating people to make effective use of the NHS, and often include advice on how to talk to your doctor.

Nearly all women's magazines include health columns with an expert who answers readers' questions. Quite frequently, the columnist addresses the issue of how to communicate with doctors. Problem pages offer interesting insights into professional relationships. If you haven't done so already, make an effort to look at the contents of a few magazines.

Research aimed at empowering patients

Roter (1979) set up a patient education programme for a group of poor women patients attending an urban out-patient department in the USA. All the women were given a preparatory tutorial in order to make them more active as patients. This 15 minute session identified the questions the patient wanted to ask and allowed her to rehearse asking them. 'The interactions with the doctor were recorded and compared with a control group who had a session about available hospital services. The prepared patients asked more questions, took a more assertive line and were more efficient in that sessions took no longer than the more passive control patients. They also improved slightly in their appointment keeping.' (p. 93)

> From this account it sounds as though the work was highly success-ful. However, there were some seemingly negative outcomes. Can you anticipate what these might have been?

Roter reported that: 'doctors judged the prepared patients as more angry and anxious and it seems that both parties were disconcerted by the more active participation obtained by this means, since established roles and styles of interaction were being challenged.' (pp. 93–94)

BOX 2.2   Generalizing to other contexts

The results of Roter's study have significance outside the doctor–patient encounter. If you were to *train* one party in an interaction (for example through individual counselling, attendance at courses or group discussions) so as to change their expectations of the other party or their definition of the situation, you would expect to find some type of imbalance in later interactions.

Suppose you were to train a group of nurses to be assertive towards doctors, or give elderly people advice on handling home helps, or send a group of woman drivers on a course to learn about cars and how to talk to car mechanics. If we think about relationships as systems, then changes in one part of the system are bound to impact on the rest of the system.

The training and orientation of doctors

Many critics say that the fundamental problem is that, after undergoing a long professional training which emphasizes biomedical issues, doctors tend to feel that they are wasting their time, their expertise and their training if they get pulled into dealing with psychological or social problems. But at the same time, more than half the graduates of UK medical schools go on to enter general practice where doctors can expect to develop long-term relationships with their patients. Moreover, it is estimated that over half of a doctor's working time is spent on problems involving primarily psychological factors, where the need is for communication skills rather than technical knowledge.

Can such skills be taught? One social psychologist, Michael Argyle, believes that it is possible to improve the social skills of healthcare professionals. Later in the course you will have the opportunity to read a paper (Reading C in Book 2) in which he outlines his ideas.

Comparing the communication skills of healthcare professionals

ACTIVITY 2.19

To what extent do these observations and criticisms apply to other healthcare professionals? Do nurses have more time to listen to patients? Are speech therapists and physiotherapists more empathetic? If you think there is a difference, how would you account for it? (Are different types of people attracted to different professions? Is the training radically different? Is the ethos of the profession different? Are the structural conditions under which clinicians operate different?)

Learning to listen

In the medical literature, a number of doctors have written about the significance of listening to the patient's story. In an article subtitled *I Can't Hear You While I'm Listening*, Richard Baron, an American doctor, gives the following account of his own behaviour:

> It happened the other morning on rounds, as it often does, that while I was carefully [listening to] a patient's chest, he began to ask me a question. 'Quiet,' I said, 'I can't hear you while I'm listening.' This typical physician–patient encounter is emblematic of a deep confusion in clinical medicine today, a confusion that seems to arise from the roots of our medical conceptualization. It is as if physicians and patients have come to inhabit different universes, and medicine, rather than being a bridge between us, has become one of the major forces keeping us apart.
>
> *(Baron, 1985, p. 606)*

Baron asks whether medicine, by taking illness from the universe of experience and moving it to a location in the physical world, has lost something: 'Having worked so hard to objectify illness, do we not have trouble confronting the fullness of the human context in which illness occurs? Have we not, in some consequential way, made disease our focus instead of sick people?' (p. 606)

The worry Baron has is that there has been a shift in focus from the human experience of illness to various technology-based facts of disease. He argues that by taking disease to be an anatomic or technologic fact, we are led further away from any ability to understand disease in human terms:

> We seem to have a great deal of difficulty taking seriously any human suffering that cannot be directly related to an anatomic or pathophysiologic derangement. It is as if this suffering had a value inferior to that associated with 'real disease' ... In a sense, we seem obliged to remove ourselves from the world of our patients in order to categorize their diseases in a technologic manner. We cannot hear them while we are listening.
>
> *(p. 607)*

What is needed is some way for doctors to re-enter the world of their patients. Doctors need to train themselves to listen and hear at the same time. Baron recommends that doctors need to be acquainted with phenomenology — an approach which seeks to reunite science with life and to explore the relationship between the abstract world of the sciences and the concrete world of human questioning.

> Of what use can all of this obscure language and metaphysics [i.e. phenomenology] be to practising physicians? It gives us a way to think about illness that allows us to take suffering as seriously as we take anatomy. ... If we can adopt a phenomenologic perspective, we can try to enter the world of illness as lived by patients rather than confining ourselves to the world of disease as described by physicians.
>
> *(p. 609)*

Negotiations between patients and healthcare professionals

As suggested at the start of this section, there is consensus as to how a medical consultation should proceed. These are that the healthcare professional should:

- talk to the person
- observe the patient
- carry out a clinical examination
- order tests
- form a hypothesis (diagnosis)
- make a prognosis
- devise a treatment plan
- if necessary, refer the patient.

Clearly the active person in the interaction is the professional. So what is the patient's role? Is the patient a passive being through all this? Since the whole purpose of the interaction is for the professional to gain as much relevant information from the patient as possible, the patient needs to verbalize his or her problems to present information to the clinician. Much of the work on communications suggests that patients want the chance to tell their story in their own terms to a sympathetic listener. They often feel constrained from doing this because they feel their role is inferior to that of the doctor. This makes them clam up, and take on a passive role.

In recent years, doctors have been interested in treating the consultation as a *negotiation process*: 'Principled medical negotiation develops trust, establishes expertise, explains treatment options fully and encourages healthy behaviour. It involves a therapeutic alliance in which conflicts are openly discussed and resolved by considering proposals from both parties.' (Thompson, 1984, p. 94)

To engage in this sort of dialogue, a patient needs information and needs to be aware of his or her rights and options, e.g. 'Do I have an automatic right to a second opinion?'; 'Can I refuse to go to hospital X?'

Empowering patients

ACTIVITY 2.20

Do you feel that you are equipped to negotiate with your GP or hospital consultant? Do you view the consultation as a negotiation process?

The last piece of research on interaction that we will examine centres around negotiation. The work is summarized in the paper 'Studies on a negotiated approach to patienthood' by Lazare et al. (1978). The setting of their research work was a North American psychiatric walk-in clinic. The team carried out interviews with several hundred patients to determine the range of patient requests in a psychiatric setting. A technique for establishing what patients expected to happen was also developed.

ACTIVITY 2.21 Negotiating with healthcare professionals

Before you read the details of this study, spend a few minutes thinking about the relevance of the concept of *negotiation* to healthcare situations. To focus your thoughts, try to think through the following issues.

1   In general, what factors might influence the negotiation process (whether in trade union situations, between partners, between parent and child, between buyer and seller)?

2   Which of these factors are relevant to negotiations between patient and healthcare professionals?

3   Who, in the patient–professional relationship, is likely to have more power in the negotiations? Why?

Feedback is given in the 'Feedback for Activities' section on page 104 of this unit.

The researchers found that what patients wanted and what they expected they would receive were not necessarily the same. For instance, a patient might need some form of counselling or therapy but expects medication. What does this mismatch mean? There are a variety of possible explanations for the fact that clients do not get what they claim they want from a professional relationship. Different psychological perspectives sensitize us to different issues. A sociologically-oriented researcher would be inclined to probe the class backgrounds of the participants and the way in which the clinic was funded. If, however, you adopted a psychodynamic perspective you would want to explore the patient's unconscious motives and conflicts. An experimental social psychologist might be interested in the patients' social skills. Although these different foci are not mutually exclusive, there is a tendency for a perspective to direct research by prioritizing the issues.

Lazare and his associates argue that the interview is a negotiation process and that elements of conflict are often present in such clinical encounters. Their research indicated that patients seeking psychiatric help *do* come with requests; 99 per cent of patients had at least one request. Whether or not these are *expressed* during the consultation, however, depends on how the clinician behaves. Their work showed that in consultations very *few* patients (37 per cent) will make these requests spontaneously. Healthcare professionals need to create circumstances in which patients feel it is safe to voice their concerns, to ask for specific help. This may entail asking patients to express their views, and making it clear that it is permissible to make requests.

If we accept that conflict is inherent in the relationship between clinician and patient, then conflict resolution by negotiation is a critical part of successful helping behaviour. If the two parties fail to negotiate successfully, the patient is likely to be dissatisfied and fail to comply with treatment recommendations, or may change doctor, complain or engage in litigation. On the clinician's part, failure to negotiate may be followed by referring the patient elsewhere or by the withholding of goodwill and support that would otherwise be offered (Lazare et al., p. 421).

Of course, clinician–patient negotiations are *not* between parties with equal power. The clinician is likely to have higher social status, greater resources, greater control over treatment alternatives, more familiarity with the role, power to refuse requests and the ability to choose the site and make the physical arrangements for the negotiations. At the same time, patients are aware of the negotiated nature of the consultation and value clinicians who possess this skill.

> We believe that the most sensitive and sought-after clinicians are the most effective negotiators. They sense the patient's worries, misconceptions about the illness, and hesitations about treatment. They create an atmosphere that encourages patients to present their perspective, on the one hand, and encourages them to hear the clinician's perspective, on the other hand. These clinicians know how to be forceful, but they also have learned how to compromise without losing their professional integrity.
>
> *(p. 422)*

As with other aspects of communication, Lazare thinks that negotiation should be taught to doctors: 'Negotiation between doctor and patient is at the heart of the clinical encounter. Yet the negotiation process is not discussed, is not taught ... and is not recorded.' (p. 424)

Research Study 3: Personal relationships and the provision of informal care

In this section we move from looking at formal relationships with healthcare professionals to a consideration of *informal care*. This material links directly to Chapter 6 of Book 2 by Dorothy Miell and Rosaleen Croghan which deals with networks of social support. It also ties in with the family life-cycle model covered by Rudi Dallos in Chapter 5 of Book 2. Chapter 6 shifts the focus from work which describes and explains social interaction and personal relationships to research which gets us to think about what individuals derive from relationships. The topic of informal care also acts as a bridge to the final part of the Trigger Unit because the expectations we have regarding social support derive, in part, from society and our cultural background.

Gillian Parker (1989, 1991, 1993), a British social researcher, has written extensively on informal care and community care. Before considering her approach to the topic and her findings, we will look at some facts and figures regarding the number of people who require care and the number of people involved in providing care.

ACTIVITY 2.22

Estimate the number of carers

What would you guess to be the number of adults in our society who provide informal care?

Feedback is given in the 'Feedback for Activities' section on page 105 of this unit.

ACTIVITY 2.23

Who helps whom?

You should answer these questions before you read the next section of the Trigger Unit.

To whom would a family be likely to turn if they needed informal (i.e. non-professional) help in caring for another family member:

- to their adult children?
- to their parents?
- to other relatives (brothers, sisters, aunts, uncles, cousins)?
- to friends?
- to neighbours?

If you were involved in providing daily care to a close relative, whom would you expect to help and support you?

What would you predict might be some of the important factors which have an impact on whom carers ask for help?

What factors are likely to constrain or limit the amount of help we feel able to give to others who are carrying a heavy burden of caring for a dependent relative?

Which of your own networks would offer the *least* help and support if you were in the position of providing caring:

- extended family?
- close family?
- neighbours?

If you yourself are involved in caring for someone, you might pose these questions to someone who does *not* have first-hand experience of caring to see whether your views differ from theirs. Conversely, if you have no direct experience of caring, try, if possible, to talk to someone who can give you insight into what is involved in caring and get them to respond to the questions in this activity.

Gillian Parker (1991, 1993) carried out in-depth interviews with 21 married couples where one partner required on-going care. Each partner was asked about the help and support they received from their children, other family members and neighbours. The work was carried out at a time when the government was committed to a policy of 'community care'. Community care may be implemented in a variety of ways ranging from comprehensive statutory provision to informal, voluntary provision. At the time she was investigating informal care, financial considerations were leading the government to look to the family to be the main care providers as highlighted in a DHSS publication, *Growing Old*:

> ... the primary sources of support and care for elderly people are informal and voluntary. These spring from the personal ties of kinship, friendship and neighbourhood ... It is the role of public authorities to sustain and, where necessary, develop — but never to displace — such support and care. Care *in* the community must increasingly mean care *by* the community.
>
> *(DHSS, 1981: para 1.9, original emphasis)*

Parker's research set out to test whether family, friends and neighbours are ready, willing and able to provide such care.

Parker's sample

When you read the material that follows you should bear in mind that Parker deliberately chose to study 21 younger (under pensionable age) couples where one partner has become disabled since marriage.

The question you should ask yourself is how this type of support compares to other types of informal caring (e.g. caring for children or helping a friend who is going through a crisis).

What follows are eleven quotations from carers in Parker's study. Imagine that you are a researcher working for Parker. These transcripts need to be analysed and turned into a research report. (Much of social psychology involves working with this type of *qualitative data*.) After you have read the material, you will be given some guidance in analysing it. Once you have made your interpretations, we will see how Parker made sense of her data.

(Note: F signifies female carer; M signifies male carer; I signifies interviewer.)

Quotation 1 (Mrs B, talking about her adult children)

F: They're very good if I need them — very, very good if I need them. But, like I say, they've got families of their own, they've got their own lives to lead and I don't put them under no obligation to do anything, but if I need help they're there.

Quotation 2 (Mr E, talking about his son)

M: Say I want him [son] to look after my wife while I do something else, he'd have to do it — but regarding anything [else], I don't think I'd bother really, I'd try and find ...

I: Find another way?

M: Yeah, find another way.

I: But it sounds as if — you'd have to be really pushed to ask him to take on some of the things you normally do?

M: I would do, yes — 'cos I don't know what it is, whether it's being pig-headed or what, I don't know really. I feel it's me duty while his mother's not well and I feel it's me duty to do it, you see, and that's it.

Quotation 3 (Mrs I, talking about her children)

F: It's not a very nice thing to see, so I mean, I try to shield them from it, I won't tell them too much, they won't ask and I won't tell. I only let them know what they've got to know at that time but beyond that, no.

Quotation 4 (Mr G, talking about his daughter)

M: It's difficult because — me daughter — she's only nine. She understands a lot of me problems and she does help in some ways but you really mean personal [care] — deep down, personal, which you can't involve your daughter in at that age.

Quotation 5 (Mrs B, talking about brothers and sisters)

F: We never really bothered each other [carer's and spouse's siblings] — I mean we all grew up together, granted, but I think as time goes by, you know, you find out you have your own responsibilities, you have your own home life. You get independent.

Quotation 6 (Mrs G, talking about her parents)

I: Do your parents help out in any sort of way?

F: Um, if I asked 'em but you see they're getting on, they're not that well themselves.

Quotation 7 (Mr J, talking about relatives)

M: I certainly wouldn't ask a relative [to help], it's too emotional a situation to ask a relative. I can put up with — a tremendous amount, I couldn't expect a relative on either side to be able to cope with that, or to do some of the physical requirements as well because, for obvious reasons, its OK for me to do it but not, you know, someone else.

Quotation 8 (Mr I, talking about neighbours)

I: Would you ever call on any of them for help or feel you could if you were stuck?

M: If it was a real emergency, a real, real emergency, yeah I would, like something happening quick and it was an emergency I would call on them.

Quotation 9 (Mrs B, talking about neighbourhood networks)

F: Once the family's grown up and left home, you get into your own environment and I think it's children that makes your relationship with neighbours more or less.

Quotation 10 (Mrs I, talking about neighbours)

F: I've been here seventeen years and I've never asked any of the neighbours to do anything for us, definitely not. I mean I've got good neighbours, they don't come in, they don't bother you, and I don't go in there.

Quotation 11 (Female carer, talking about neighbours)

I: You don't get any [help] from neighbours ... friends?

F: No, he wouldn't let them ...

I: He wouldn't?

F: No. No, he wouldn't let them. In fact he gets so embarrassed that I have to do it. First thing on a morning he says, 'Put me socks on, put me slippers on, before anybody comes in'. He doesn't like to think that anybody knows what I have to do for him you see.

Analysing the interview data

ACTIVITY 2.25

Now go back through the quotations, and undertake the following activities.

1 Identify the key themes in each quote and enter them into the matrix below.

2 Group the quotes, using whatever criterion you think is relevant.

3 Write up your conclusions about informal care and the implications for community care. (This could be in the form of a list of ideas.)

Table 2 Data matrix for analysis of interview material

Quotation	Themes
1	
2	
3	
4	
5	
6	
7	
8	
9	
10	
11	

Parker's interpretation of the data

Here is a summary of Parker's interpretations and conclusions.

1   Adult children on the whole did *not* provide substantial practical help or support to their parents. The reasons why children did not offer much help were connected to different types of constraints.

Objective constraints	Subjective constraints
• distance • lack of adequate resources • demands of their own job • had their own problems (e.g. divorce, unemployment, poor health)	• parents did not expect children to help out • carer's belief that it was their duty to care • need to reserve help for emergencies • parents unwillingness to ask for help • shame, embarrassment — desire to protect children from full knowledge of the disability

Parker identifies another set of constraining factors which concern age, gender, and the nature of the caring task. Young children were less likely to be involved than were older ones. And, regardless of their age, boys were not seen as sources of help.

2   In all, only half the couples mentioned any form of help or support received from their extended family. Only one couple had any kind of extended kinship network that was capable of delivering, or willing to deliver, help on a regular basis. With other family members the type of help received was mostly with transport and household maintenance rather than with caring or domestic tasks. The constraints on help from other kin were distance and competing responsibilities.

3   Parents were a more acceptable source of help than were children. There was not the same degree of reluctance to accept or request help from parents as there was from offspring.

> This apparently easy reassertion of the parent–child relationship seems important, and is suggested in other work on disablement in adulthood ... Further, work on children caring for their elderly parents has shown how difficult it can be to reverse the 'normal' direction of caregiving. ... when dependency *starts* in old age, there is an 'expectation', not always mutual, that children will take on caring responsibilities. By contrast, when dependency starts before old age, carers and spouses may look more easily to their own parents for help.
>
> (p. 189)

The main constraint to parents helping their children was their own frailty or ill health. In many cases, ageing parents placed an additional burden on carers.

4   Those who are not involved in day-to-day care are unable to understand what is involved.

5   Carers and their dependants often seek to present a brave front to the world and to disguise the work involved and the degree of dependency.

6   Carers often feel guilty at not being able to give help to other people, especially older members of their own family.

> This perceived 'failure' to help others is very important because, as we already know, reciprocity is an important factor in the maintenance of helping networks ... When people are unable to *give* the help that they feel they should be giving they are correspondingly uneasy about *receiving* help. This then leads, in part at least, to the determined stance of independence to which so many of the couples clung. This independence — we keep ourselves to ourselves — and the whole process by which couples come to it, contribute to a weakening of kinship networks.
>
> *(p. 191)*

7   Neighbourhood networks are rarely a source of help and support with the burden of caring. Obviously, proximity is a 'given' regarding neighbours, so why do they play such an insignificant role in the lives of those who are engaged in caring for a partner? Parker explores various reasons why the neighbourhood network is not a resource for most carers.

Lack of neighbourhood support

ACTIVITY 2.26

Before you read Parker's speculations, spend a few minutes thinking about this and write down your own ideas.

The reasons given for neighbours not helping were, Parker found, broadly similar to those advanced for children and other relatives. But there were additional factors linked to lack of neighbourly help.

* *Disengagement from the local community and neighbourhood* — Parker identified a number of factors which led to a lack of contact with neighbours:

    – moving to a new neighbourhood

    – former neighbours and friends moving away

    – restricted opportunities for establishing new networks and relationships because of the demands of caring and the limitations of disablement

    – lack of opportunities to meet neighbours once children have grown up.

* *Generational factors* — If neighbours are elderly, they are no more able to provide help than the respondents with caring responsibilities are to give it. On the other hand, young neighbours are likely to be pre-

occupied with their own lives and older couples probably feel that they do not have anything in common with younger neighbours.

- *Attitudinal issues* —Notions of what constitutes 'good' neighbouring seem to be very influential in determining neighbourly networks. Attitudes such as 'keeping yourself to yourself' and respecting boundaries are incompatible with the idea that a good neighbour is someone who is concerned with one's welfare and who is prepared to help out from time to time. In the case of some of the couples in Parker's sample, boundaries were kept deliberately high out of a need or wish to protect the spouse.

Parker offers some very interesting insights into the way in which age, illness and involvement with neighbours interact.

> This combination of the presence of young children and the time and opportunity to reciprocate neighbourly help is, of course, of enormous importance in regard to couples who are young at the time of the onset of disability or illness. Those whose children are grown have had the opportunity to make links with their neighbours in the normal way. If they remain in the same neighbourhood, even if everyone grows old and frail together, they do, at least, retain a sense of belonging. By contrast, younger married couples, when the disability or illness starts before their dependent children have grown, have neither the time nor the opportunity to make these normal links. This leaves them reliant on help from their family … Only if younger married couples can replace neighbourly networks with networks (such as membership of a church or chapel) which do not necessarily depend on reciprocity do they stand any chance of receiving informal help from outside the family.
>
> *(pp. 194–5)*

ACTIVITY 2.27

Mapping the quotations to the analysis

Spend a few minutes looking again at the quotations and see whether they map to Parker's analysis. Are there any quotations which do not seem to fit? Are there additional themes which you've identified but which Parker omits?

Generalizing to other cultures

Suppose you were to repeat Parker's survey with a sample from a different racial or religious background or to replicate it in another country. Do you think that your results would be different if you studied:

- a sample from an Irish community living in the UK?
- a Greek Cypriot sample living in the UK?
- an Orthodox Jewish sample living in the UK?
- a West Indian sample living in the UK?
- a Bangladeshi sample living in the UK?

Feedback is given in the 'Feedback for Activities' section on page 105 of this unit.

Here is Parker's summing up: '… this group of carers and the people they care for have no or only residual networks of family and neighbours which *could* be activated to help them. Even if they do have networks, they are not at all keen that these *should* be used to help.' (p. 195)

What she concludes from her study is that we need to be wary of the assumption that informal networks can or should be depended upon to provide the help needed by the group she studied. This does not mean that informal support networks do not exist. What Parker does call into question is the assumption in much of recent policy that there is a large potential reserve of helpers waiting to be called upon — kin, neighbours, friends.

In answer to the question 'Can (and should) informal networks provide informal care?', Parker says that her own research on non-elderly carers and their disabled or chronically ill spouses: '… calls into serious question whether such help could be activated for this and other groups. It also raises doubts about whether such help would be acceptable to dependent people or their carers.' (p. 185)

Your views   ACTIVITY 2.28

Do you agree with Parker's conclusion? Does it accord with your own experience and your reading of her interview material?

If Parker is correct, then what implications does this have for community care?

Additional reading

This review of Parker's work in section 2 was extremely selective. Items have been chose to act as a *trigger* for D317. If you are interested in the topic, I recommended that you read her book, *With This Body: Caring and Disability in Marriage* (1992), which provides a succinct and lucid report of the study.

There is a growing literature on the link between social support and health. If you want to follow this up, here are a few suggestions.

Chapter 2, 'A friend a day keeps the doctor away: social support and health', of Oakley's book *Social Support and Motherhood: The Natural History of a Research Project* (1992) traces the growing interest in social support and the concomitant consumer dissatisfaction with the medical model. This is an excellent starting point for anyone wanting an orientation to the area or ideas for a research project.

A general review of the field can be found in Gore (1989) 'Social networks and social supports in health care' in Freeman, H.E. and Levine, S. (eds.), *Handbook of Medical Sociology*. The paper contains a very extensive set of references; the end of the paper looks at policy issues.

Review of Section 2

This second part of the Trigger Unit has covered a good deal of ground. In looking at personal relationships as a domain of social psychological research we have reviewed the following material.

- The different methods of studying social interaction. We sketched out six different methods: direct observation, retrospective interviews, group discussions, document analysis, review of complaints and litigation, and experiments.

- The suggestion that social actors may operate with diverse interpretations of a social situation such as a medical consultation. We looked in particular at Cornwell's work on public and private accounts.

- The way that different social psychological perspectives emphasize different facets of social interaction and personal relationships, (e.g. an experimental social skills model compared to a psychodynamic model).

- The gradual shift in the way in which researchers study social interaction, with a greater willingness to adopt an 'inside' perspective.

- The negotiated nature of social life: there is growing awareness among clinicians of the need to acknowledge the patient's perspective, to negotiate a shared understanding of the patient's problem and the best way of managing it.

- The way in which power differentials influence interactions between professionals and clients.

- The reasons why informal social networks do not provide substantial support to carers.

3 Situating health and illness in a sociocultural context

Introduction

The goal of the first part of this Trigger Unit was to explore personal experiences of health and illness and the way in which social psychological perspectives may provide different interpretations of personal accounts. In the second part our attention switched to interpersonal relations centring around the giving and receiving of care. We looked firstly at ways of researching the forms of relationships which develop between patients and healthcare professionals (e.g. passivity, compliance, dependency); we also considered social and psychological factors which limit the amount of social support available to informal carers.

In this concluding section we will look at the way in which conceptions and experiences of health and illness are embedded in a broader social context. In the course of this exploration we will consider the way in which healthcare professionals are recruited and socialized to play their roles, how images of health and illness are generated and transmitted and the way in which health care as a social institution gives rise to conflicts and tensions. We will draw on the work of medical sociologists and anthropologists, as well as social psychologists. The coverage of this final section will anticipate the domain of Book 3 of the course (*Identities, Groups and Social Issues*).

Our method of approach will be similar to the way in which we handled the first two domains. You will be asked to formulate the types of questions which interest you; we will then consider methods of translating such questions into a systematic method of investigation; we will consider what social psychological perspectives might be relevant; and finally we will look at examples of work which focus on social-cultural issues.

The influence of social and cultural factors on health and illness   ACTIVITY 3.1

See if you can identify four or five ways in which individual or interpersonal experiences of health or illness may be structured by broader social processes (such as groups, group process, social structures and organizations, institutions or culture).

Feedback is given in the 'Feedback for Activities' section on page 106 of this unit.

3.1 The recruitment and socialization of healthcare professionals

Earlier in this unit we looked at interactions between patients (or healthcare consumers) and healthcare professionals. We now want to step back from the individuals involved in these encounters and find out what occurs during professional training to prepare individuals to deal with other people's illness. In particular, we want to discover how social groups and institutions influence the way qualified individual clinicians come to define their role.

Before we delve into research about professional socialization, we need to think about who gains entry to professional training.

Entry into medicine

Chapter 5 of Book 3 uses work and employment to develop ideas about the relationship between individuals and institutions. One of the topics Diane Watson (the chapter author) raises is how individuals choose the work they do.

ACTIVITY 3.2

Why do individuals choose to study medicine or nursing?

Make a list of the reasons why an individual might decide to study medicine or nursing.

What reasons are candidates likely to give to the interview panel when asked why they are seeking entry to medicine or nursing?

Feedback is given in the 'Feedback for Activities' section on page 107 of this unit.

In her chapter, Watson is sceptical about occupational choice research which emphasizes either individual *choice* or the *constraints* imposed by circumstance. Her objections derive from her rejection of the implied models of the person which underlie the dichotomy that either we exercise free will or we are the passive victims of our social world. There is a sense in which the very notion of choosing a career is misleading because it overlooks the extent to which social class factors influence the occupations people enter. Does this apply to medicine? Sheila Lowry (1993) in her book on medical education notes that British medical schools have had little success in ensuring a mix of social class backgrounds:

> The social class mix of British medical students has changed little in the past 30 years, and the latest figures available ... confirm that 31 per cent of applicants and 38 per cent of acceptances in 1991 came from professional families (the corresponding figures for skilled manual

workers and unskilled workers being 8 per cent and 7 per cent and 0.7 per cent and 0.4 per cent respectively). Recent trends like the student loan scheme and the recession will further discourage applicants from poorer backgrounds.

(p. 16)

These data confirm the view that social class and educational background place people in 'varying degrees of proximity with different ease of access' to various kinds of occupation and employment (Roberts, 1975, as quoted in Watson). But there is a danger, as Watson points out, that in rejecting the notion that individuals make occupational choices in line with their self-image, we will be pushed towards an equally one-sided and over-deterministic approach which focuses exclusively on structural constraints. This would lead us to assume that individual factors are *totally* irrelevant. As you will discover when you read Watson's chapter, some theorists maintain that it is possible to develop accounts which give equal weight to individual action and social structure.

Bennett (1987) in his fascinating book on how medicine as a career impacts upon individuals, provides an account of why he chose to study medicine which would seem to support Watson's claim that both agency and structure play a part. He cites both class background and his own appraisal of where he would best fit: 'Why did *I* study medicine? ... There were immediate reasons largely determined by my middle-class professional background which ordained a career in one of the professions.' (p. 85)

For Bennett, selecting medicine was a process of elimination: 'My first step in selecting a career ... was to avoid being dispatched into the army. That left the church, the law and medicine. I had no leaning towards the church and was not thought strong enough at classics for the law, so medicine was the choice.' (p. 85)

Bennett goes on to show how his understanding of medicine was influenced by his father who was a psychiatrist. In looking back at how he viewed his father, Bennett provides us with a very powerful image of the life-style of a successful doctor before the Second World War:

> My father was always busy on important matters. He went out early in the day and returned late; and at weekends the house had to be quiet because he was working. He was highly successful in his practice, which was largely private, as was the way in the 1930s and the 1940s after the war; he was in great demand, so had little time for his family — even if he had the inclination to spend time with small children. He was seldom there but he dominated the household. So what does all this amount to? What message was being given to my brother and me about the profession of medicine? Whatever else it was, it was clear that medicine was an important activity: people respected doctors and deferred to them. The doctor's business came

first, and it was apparent that the doctor always got his own way. The cynic might say it was a well-rewarded way of doing just as one pleased, but it was hard work and chancy.

(p. 86)

Despite the fact that a high proportion of medical students come from 'medical' families, Bennett does not subscribe to the view that only one type of person ends up choosing to study medicine. (However, he does seem to think that certain 'personality characteristics' are found in successful consultants and in ambitious students.)

Professional socialization

What goes on in medical school or in nursing college to prepare students to assume a professional role? Obviously, students spend much time acquiring biomedical facts. They learn in great detail about how the human body functions and about the pathology of disease. As well as theoretical knowledge, they also learn clinical skills: how to talk to patients, examine them, carry out various tests, and procedures. But professional training involves more than just learning facts and learning how to do things. There is a *socialization process* going on at the same time which shapes students' attitudes, beliefs and values.

This process is subtle and the end result varies from one individual to the next. Graduates from medical colleges or nursing schools clearly do not emerge with a rigid set of values or ways of dealing with patients. Some individuals find an easy fit between their personal values and the values promulgated by their institution. For others, there is ongoing tension. Furthermore, the process of socialization may itself alter over time, as the social organization of health care is restructured.[3] Finally, the process needs to be viewed alongside the types of individuals who are attracted to a career in medicine and the types of candidates from this potential pool who are selected.

In looking at the process of socialization into a profession or an occupation we have the opportunity to view the processes through which individuals are integrated and incorporated into institutions. Book 3 argues that this is a two-way process in that the institution seeks to shape the individual who, in turn, works to construct and create social structures.

If there is a misfit between personal values and the values which the institution seems to reward, what happens? How do individuals experience institutional or group pressure? Are they able to resist the pressure of peer groups or their tutors? As we shall see when we look at the pro-

---

[3]At the time of writing this unit, the NHS reforms and the closing of teaching hospitals has sparked debate about the need for a more community-oriented medical education. This is turn raises questions as to whether certain recruits to medical school would feel more at home in community settings rather than in traditional teaching hospitals.

cess of socialization into the culture of medical schools, under these circumstances it is rarely a simple matter of conforming to social norms, of discarding key elements of one's personal identity in order to take on a new social identity or of outright rebellion against authority. Identities are not like clothes which can be put on or removed at will. Yet, it would be surprising if prolonged exposure to a set of institutional values did not have some impact on personal identity.

Investigating professional socialization   ACTIVITY 3.3

Before sampling some of the work which has been done on professional socialization, spend a few minutes thinking about how you might study this topic. Make a list of some of the questions you would like to investigate.

If you are a healthcare professional, spend a few moments reflecting on your own training. Try to recall whether, during training, efforts were made to mould your attitudes and values. Did your training involve a reshaping of your personality, a discarding of an earlier self? And how important was your peer group in this process?

If you are *not* a healthcare professional, you might consider at what points in their training student nurses and doctors are most likely to have their attitudes and values challenged. Try to imagine what aspects of patient care or interaction with clinicians might be most embarrassing, upsetting or distasteful to an 18-year-old student.

Research on the socialization of medical students

In the UK, students embarking on a medical degree arrive with at least eighteen years of life experience. Although these students are not a cross-section of the population, nonetheless, they bring with them quite varied life histories. How is it that, starting with this quite heterogeneous collection of individuals, with their own beliefs and opinions, a common social role and a social identity (*the doctor*) is formed? A number of classic research studies have tracked students throughout their medical studies to try to answer this question. The key work was carried out by American sociologists (Merton et al., 1957; Becker et al., 1961; Fox, 1974). The authors of these reports believe that, in the course of their studies, students not only acquire knowledge and skills, but also values, attitudes and behaviour patterns which go to making up the doctor's professional role.

The significance of this work in the context of Book 3 of D317 is that it should get you thinking about the nature of *social identity*. As used by Margaret Wetherell (the Book 3 editor) this phrase refers to the parts of a person's biography concerned with his or her group membership and position in society. One of the themes in the first chapter of the book is the importance of groups and group processes in forging and maintaining different kinds of social identity. Another important focus in Book 3 is the way in which structuring principles which are 'out there' in society, become translated into the way in which individuals live their lives. In the context of medical training, what we want to understand is how various features of the professional role to which students are exposed are reproduced in the next generation of doctors.

Studies which focus on the process of induction into medicine or nursing also serve to illustrate some of the themes developed by Helen Morgan and Kerry Thomas in Chapter 2 of Book 3. Unconscious factors, they argue, influence groups as well as individuals. Just as individual anxiety gives rise to various defence mechanisms, the same process occurs at the group level. (The psychodynamic perspective is applied in their chapter to a study of hospital nurses.)

Research by social scientists and medical educationalists suggest that medical students collectively experience a great deal of anxiety. Can we find any evidence of group defences? Does the culture of medical school serve as a defence against anxiety? Some of the research evidence reported later in this section could readily be interpreted in this way.

Training for detached concern

Medical students arrive at medical school with high ideals about helping people, and are taken aback by some of the attitudes of senior clinicians (Bennett, 1987). Far from being concerned and caring, staff seem able to distance themselves from the sufferings and concerns of their patients. Students feel under pressure from older students and from tutors to learn to suppress their emotions and to develop detached concern for patients. The early studies on professional socialization tried to make sense of how students coped with such pressures, how they attempted to unify their personal values with what were perceived as the role requirements. Attention focused on the way in which students attained 'detached concern' and how they managed to overcome social taboos.

Fox (1974a) defines 'detached concern' as 'the process by which students gradually learn to combine the counter-attitudes of detachment and concern to attain the balance between objectivity and empathy expected of mature physicians.' (p. 56)

Students must know when it is appropriate to regard the human body with the impersonal attitude of scientists and when they are required to maintain some degree of sensitivity to the human implications of what they are doing.

Learning to break taboos

Harper (1993) gives the following account of the taboos that doctors in training must learn to break: '[Doctors] touch the living and dissect the dead. We probe the body's orifices and make new ones. We become familiar with the bodily effluvia. We ask strangers to undress so that we may look at and touch their bodies. We cause pain.' (p. 913)

From the point of view of social psychology, the way in which students negotiate these experiences provides insight into the way in which social pressures and expectations (from the peer group and key authority figures) make it possible to overcome social inhibitions.

To summarize, medical training involves a transition from raw recruits to insiders who have broken the taboos surrounding illness, nakedness, sex and death. Starting at an average age of twenty-one, students are required to learn to ask patients intimate questions about their bodily functions, deal with anger and grief, and perform difficult procedures under pressure. As one final year student said 'You feel that you've touched on everything that was ever held private or sacred and nothing is sacred any more. The human body loses any mystique it ever had' (p. 90).

British evidence: the 'Doctors To Be' series

A BBC series (*Doctors To Be*) made in the mid-1980s looked at ten students at St Mary's Hospital in Paddington, London, over seven years. Eight programmes were made and over 300 hours of material were recorded. The material selected for this section focuses on the subculture of the medical school: how new students are inducted into this culture and how the subculture comes to act as the reference group (Spindler, 1992).

The culture of medical schools

One of the striking features of medical schools is the type of humour which pervades student culture. To outsiders the culture of medical schools may seem crude, barbaric, immature and sexist. Students are frequently initiated into this culture through various ritual events. At St Mary's, the tradition at the time the television programmes were made was for students to receive a spoof lecture on their first day. This was given by a doctor with a pyjama-clad 'patient' on a trolley, accompanied by a nurse.

After reading the account that follows of this first year spoof lecture, spend a few minutes thinking about the significance of this event. Why do you think that such rituals are built into medical education? What messages are first year students likely to take away from this experience?

ACTIVITY 3.4

The humour was typical medical revue fare: rude and crude. A succession of first years were summoned from the audience to assist in the examination of the young male patient. One had to hold up a number plate to test the patient's sight; it said EEG I (a reference to the number plate of Dr Thomas's Rolls Royce) but the patient read PENI 5 — to a roar of laughter. Another tested the patient's reflexes by applying a vibrator to his bare foot. The patient was copiously 'sick' (a convincing cocktail of water and chopped vegetables) over a girl who examined his throat too energetically, prompting Dr Thomas to stress the importance of white coats. [One male student] was asked to find out whether diabetes was present by tasting a specimen of urine for its sugariness.

[A female student] was another victim: she was invited to examine the patient, who removed his shirt to reveal a lacy black bra and suspender belt. 'Do you notice anything wrong with this patient?' demanded Dr Thomas. Jane shook her head. 'No? Well for Paddington that is quite normal,' he conceded and asked Jane to test the man's abdominal reflex with a sharp object. She usèd her fingernails and what began as an examination ended as a caress, with the patient beaming with pleasure.

The audience rocked with laughter throughout the lecture.

(Spindler, 1992, p. 29)

Were you shocked by the fact that new students would be expected to witness, and perhaps take part in, such an event on their first day? What possible function could this event have? What lessons would students learn? Can you see how this might be construed as part of a socialization process? What follows is the interpretation given by Susan Spindler, the producer of the series.

Jokes which focus on the uncomfortable similarity between feeling someone's abdomen and stroking it for pleasure are perhaps especially potent for a group of people who spend their professional lives walking that tightrope every time they see a patient. For the older students in the audience, testing urine, genital examinations, questions about patient's sex lives, were all familiar territory. They laughed the loudest. The novices joined in, some with bewilderment, others with embarrassment. Their initiation was under way.

(p. 29)

One students made the following observation about the culture of medical schools:

It's like a club ... You only get the jokes because you're part of the medical profession, people outside don't understand them ... The humour is notoriously about medical situations we have all been in ... The crudity and jokes about the body come from an overfamiliarity with human anatomy: we're dealing all day with things that are taboo for normal people to talk about and we discuss them without batting an eyelid. And that breeds jokes.

(pp. 111–12)

When you read Book 3, you will have a chance to contrast the role of humour in a medical school with its function in a factory setting.

Coping with human dissection

The experience of medical students in the anatomy laboratory has always been viewed as a *rite de passage*. This is the place where students first encounter death. Dissection is an introduction to the professional privilege of intervention in the human body and is part of the socialization for the doctor's role. It is also a test as to how one will measure up against one's peers.

Coping mechanisms

ACTIVITY 3.5

Try to imagine how students cope with this part of their studies. What individual and group coping mechanisms would you expect them to use?

At St Mary's weekly dissection classes were attended by the whole year. A hundred students together somehow made it easier for them to overcome 'their natural inhibitions about cutting into dead human flesh. With the whole group engaged in the activity, it was, curiously enough, more comfortable for individuals to conform and get on with it than to run away in revulsion.' (p. 47)

Bizarre as it may seem to an outsider, within a short time, dissection sessions become an event which most students, far from dreading, look forward to. According to one student: 'Anatomy is a great social event because it is the only time in the week when the whole year is together in one room in a situation where they can wander round and chat to one another.' (p. 48)

So one coping mechanism is to become engrossed in the scientific, technical and learning tasks at hand. Students strive to cultivate scientific detachment because they fear that 'an overly emotional reaction to lab, whether or not it is publicly expressed, will signify to them or to others that they are unfit to become physicians.' Dissection of a human cadaver is seen by students as a test of one's emotional competence to become a doctor. Students strive to keep emotional equilibrium in the face of deeply stirring experiences. Thus, dealing with dissection is part of the preparation for the 'ethic of stoicism' that is at the core of the school's culture. Cadaver stories form part of the anticipatory socialization of students.

Although students learn to cope with dissection, there is disagreement in the literature as to the emotional significance of working with a cadaver. Some have taken the view that students adapt quickly and settle down to a professional, work-centred experience. The cadaver becomes a 'specimen' or machine on which necessary learning takes place. Others (e.g. Hafferty, 1991; Fox, 1974b) think this construction glosses over important differences. They maintain that how students handle the experience (the tensions, ambiguities and ambivalences concerning feelings) lays the groundwork for attitudes towards patients in later professional situations. Hafferty sees socialization as a conscious strategy, rooted in a 'structure of norms about feelings and their management within the emergent subculture of medical training'.

Changing identities

Professional training involves a metamorphosis, a slow transformation from being a member of the public to being a member of the medical profession. In the early days of their clinical studies, students find themselves confused about their role — although they are apprentice 'doctors-to-be', they often sympathize with the point of view of the patients and nurses. For example, they may feel depressed by the plight of geriatric patients or psychiatric patients. They may experience conflicting loyalties, sensing they have more in common with patients and their families than with healthcare professionals: 'There is a continual tension in the role of a medical student. You are slowly moving from being an ignorant member of the public to being a member of the clan with all the inside information, and you're halfway there, which is always a dangerous position to be in.' (Spindler, 1992, p. 93)

Over time, students experience a shift in their identity: 'As the clinical course continued, the gap between our students and the patients they saw in clinics and on the wards widened. They began to develop a more professional manner, still friendly but also reserved, which enabled them to distance themselves from the suffering they saw around them.' (p. 105)

Students themselves are aware of how hard it is to tread the path between empathy and professional objectivity: 'I have to learn to control myself, to realize that this is work and not let it affect me emotionally. We get some guidance from the course about how to take things step by step, which helps you get the work done, but it doesn't help you to stop feeling.' (Medical student, quoted by Spindler, 1992, p. 94)

Six months later, this same student relates how she has begun to deal with such problems: 'It's a matter of experience and learning that the world is not as pleasant a place as one had always thought. I cried a lot at first, but I wouldn't sit down and cry at a particularly sad case now. I've changed.' (pp. 94–95)

The student recognized the way in which she has altered since she began her course. She sensed that she was beginning to see patients as a separate thing from persons. She felt she had become a harder person, but deemed that this was probably necessary and inevitable. She had internalized the idea that doctors must be emotionally tough in order to get on with their work.

ACTIVITY 3.6   **Relevance to other professions**

To what extent do these same learning processes take place in other professions? Do lawyers and accountants experience such dilemmas and conflicts? I suspect that it is far more likely that the type of socialization which has been so vividly described in relation to medicine occurs in other caring or healing profession e.g. social work and nursing.

There is an on-going debate within medical schools as to whether we want future doctors to develop in this way. In his work, Fox noted a shift about half-way through medical school. Students' difficulties in relating to patients altered from what they had previously experienced as *too much concern* to that of *too much detachment.* Many students go through a period of emotional numbness. However, he sensed that this phase of hyperdetachment was only temporary.

Other researchers have not been so sanguine. Becker and his colleagues (1961) for example argued that what medical school does is to destroy or undermine youthful idealism, putting in its place a cynical or jaded view of patients.

Changing the ethos and curriculum of medical schools

In the mid-1990s there is growing recognition of the need for radical reform in medical schools. In 1993 the General Medical Council issued a document, *Tomorrow's Doctors,* which made recommendations for improving undergraduate medical education. Medical schools through-out the country have studied these recommendations with a view to modifying their courses.

Many schools have already initiated changes. Death, caring for termi-nally ill patients, and breaking bad news have started to be addressed in the clinical curriculum, along with courses on medical ethics. Counselling services for students are being introduced. Another import-ant innovation has been a move to introduce what is called community-based medicine. The philosophy behind such courses is to get students to see patients as people (or as partners) by introducing them to health service users outside medical settings e.g. in their own homes or in com-munity settings.

3.2   Medicine as culture

At various points in the Trigger Unit, reference has been made to ways in which individuals structure their experience or try to understand their social worlds. From the very beginning, one of the central ques-tions for social psychology has been that of trying to understand *how*, to put it crudely, *society gets inside our heads.* In the history of the disci-pline, a range of concepts have been proposed as mediating devices between individuals and social collectives. Attitudes (sets of enduring individual preferences and evaluations) were one such device. Social representations (images shared by members of a social group) are a more recent attempt to try to account for shared views. Jonathan Potter in Chapter 3 of Book 3 traces the history of these two concepts and argues that there are problems with both. He makes the case for abandoning attitudes and social representations and looking to what is called discursive psychology to understand the way in which people construct versions of the world. Discursive psychology concerns itself with the way in which people go about constructing and defending a believable version of the world and, at the same time, a believable version of the self.

In this section we shall look at the case that has been made to incorporate these ideas into the study of health and illness. Lupton (1994) is one writer who suggests that social constructionism is emerging as a dominant perspective for engaging in inquiries into the sociocultural dimensions of medicine, health and disease. This section will try to convey some of the key features of Lupton's thesis.

Lupton points to the increasing attention paid by social scientists to language and discursive processes in the production and maintenance of social life and subjectivity. You have already met this perspective in the first part of the Trigger Unit when we discussed individual accounts of health and illness. To remind you, the essence of social constructionism lies in the assumption that 'human subjects are viewed as being constituted in and through discourses and social practices which have complex histories ... "truth" should be considered the product of power relations, and as such, is never neutral, but always acting in the interests of someone.' (Lupton, 1994, p. 11)

Where does this lead us in the field of health and illness? According to Lupton: 'The social constructionist approach does not necessarily call into question the reality of disease or illness states or bodily experiences, it merely emphasizes that these states and experiences are known and interpreted via social activity and therefore should be examined using cultural and social analysis.' (p. 11)

Perhaps the most startling claim put forward by Lupton is the idea that rather than regarding medical knowledge as an incremental progression towards a more refined and better knowledge (the orthodox view of scientific progress), it would be more useful to see it as 'a series of relative constructions which are dependent upon the socio-historical settings in which they occur and are constantly renegotiated.' (p. 11)

What follows from this way of thinking about medicine is the conclusion that the claims of biomedicine are as much *social products* as is lay knowledge of health and illness.

ACTIVITY 3.7   **Is medical knowledge socially constructed?**

The notion that medical knowledge is socially constructed may well strike a discordant note which contradicts all that you know and believe about scientific medicine. Can you think of two or three arguments to refute the claim that medicine is a social product?

Are you able to think of evidence which might substantiate this claim?

Feedback is given in the 'Feedback for Activities' section on page 108 of this unit.

The case for viewing medicine as a cultural artefact (rather than an objective body of scientific knowledge which stands outside culture) stems from the fact that people construct their understandings of the world, including their beliefs about medicine and disease, from their interaction with cultural products as well as personal experience and discussions with others. (This assertion applies to clinicians and medical scientists as well as consumers of medicine.)

In our society, one of the most important cultural products is the mass media:

> The mass media are important in portraying medicine, health care, disease, illness and health risks in certain ways, from the soap opera's kindly doctor to the news bulletin's account of medical miracles, contributing to people's understanding of these phenomena, especially when they have little or no direct experience of them. It is clear that medicine, health care, illness and the doctor–patient relationship are cultural activities and experiences, and as such, are appropriate areas of study for sociologists of culture and scholars in the field of cultural studies. [*And, we would add, social psychologists.*] Furthermore, the study of the ways in which medical practices and institutions are represented in the mass media and the reception of such representations by audiences is integral to interpretative scholarship attempting to understand the socio-cultural aspects of medicine and health-related knowledges and practices.
>
> *(Lupton, 1994, p. 17)*

3.3 Social psychology and the study of the mass media

Translating Lupton's agenda to the discipline of social psychology, the argument would be that we need to study the way in which the mass media present biomedical information, the propensity of different social groups to seek out such information and the way in which individuals incorporate public discourse into their own world views. In addition, one might want to explore how (or whether) exposure to the stream of information and images with which the mass media bombard us day in and day out influences our behaviour or our life-styles.

Is this research programme do-able? Does it fall within the province of social psychology? If we look at the long involvement of social psychologists in studying persuasion and communication (including the mass media), then clearly social psychology long ago staked a claim to this field of research.

Although social psychology has had a long history of studying the mass media, the questions posed by social constructionists are quite different from the orientation of the earlier traditions, most of which were concerned to establish causal relationships between viewing behaviour and subsequent attitudes and behaviour. Because of their focus on individuals, the classic social psychological work in this area was not concerned with social images or representations *per se*. The work of the French social psychologist, Serge Moscovici, in the 1970s, broadened the study of the mass media and created an interest in understanding the nature of social representations and the role of the media in creating or disseminating such images. Jonathan Potter in Chapter 3 of Book 3 summarizes this work and presents a case study of Claudine Herzlich's pioneering work which applied social representation theory to the study of health and illness. He also discusses what he takes to be the limitations to social representation theory.

BOX 3.1   Social psychological research on the mass media

Social psychological studies on the mass media have tended to be driven by a concern to deal with pressing social problems. One important strand of work dates from communication research initiated during World War Two to study the impact of propaganda and the effectiveness of campaigns designed to mobilize public opinion.

The second important tradition was concerned with assessing the impact of the mass media on individual members of an audience. Because of the funding and the social concerns of the time, a major preoccupation was to determine whether observing violence and aggression had a harmful effect on children and adolescents (research which was discussed in DSE202).

One recurrent criticism of this work was that much of it was concerned with isolating *individual* responses to the mass media.

ACTIVITY 3.8

Content analysis of a magazine or popular television drama

In our society we are bombarded with messages about health and illness. To focus your attention on the way in which such issues are constructed, we suggest that you carry out *one* of the following exercises:

Exercise 1: Analysis of the contents of a women's magazine[4]

Select a recent copy of a woman's magazine and go through it page by page, counting how many of the feature items deal with health or illness (or mention health); do the same for advertisements. You might note any

---

[4]Although I'm tempted to include men's magazines, at the time of preparing this unit, men's magazines do not devote as much space to health issues as do women's magazines. There is an exception – a newly launched magazine devoted to men's health, but it is uncertain whether this publication will survive. If you wish, you could compare magazines aimed at men with those which target women to see if you can detect differences in their treatment of health issues.

overlap between articles which deal with health/beauty and health. Eliott (1994) presents a content analysis of the way women's magazines deal with health issues.

(You may already have material in your Resource File which you can analyse.)

Exercise 2: Analysis of a popular TV drama

Select an episode of a series set in a hospital. As you watch the programme, list the themes portrayed and the underlying human or ethical issues raised.

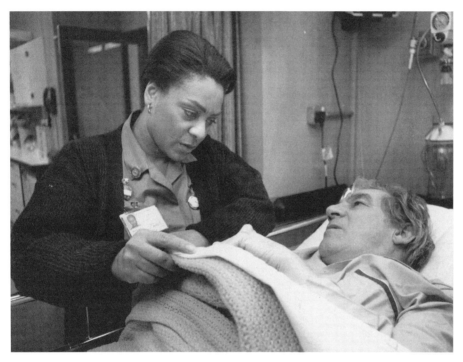

A scene from 'Casualty' — one of the many popular television programmes set in a hospital environment. Why is the public so fascinated by hospital drama?

In the context of the Trigger Unit we will look briefly at Anne Karpf's work which examines the role of the mass media in conveying images of health, illness and medicine.

In her book, *Doctoring the Media: the Reporting of Health and Medicine,* (1988), Karpf sought to demonstrate how the official medical perspective dominates the media's coverage of health and illness 'in spite of greater diversity in the media's reporting of health and medical issues … medical definitions and perceptions still prevail, and squeeze out more contentious, oppositional viewpoints which take an environmental approach and look at the politics of health.' (p. 2)

One consequence of excluding or marginalizing other perspectives, Karpf argues, is that the media plays a significant part in narrowing public debate about health, illness and medicine. Her book seeks to analyse the ways in which medicine, as a social and ideological force, is fortified and amplified by the mass media, along with other cultural institutions.

Karpf paints a picture of an uneasy relationship between the medical profession and the mass media. In the early days of television, the majority of doctors believed that 'it was wrong to submit medicine to television's gaze in any way, that a little public learning was a dangerous thing, and that anxiety and hypochondria would ripple through the audience.' (p. 4)

But since those early days the medical profession has learned to live with 'the box', and have attempted to manipulate it to their own ends. This does not, however, mean that they have always been successful. As Karpf reports, the main contemporary medical criticism of the media is that it is alarmist and sensationalist, fanning controversy. In addition, the media is often accused of gunning for the medical profession and the medicine it practises, conducting a 'trial by television'. At the heart of this conflict between the profession and the media, says Karpf, lies the medical profession's hostility to images of medicine which differ significantly from its own. Any such deviations are likely to be labelled as distortions or bias. The British Medical Association's view on the ideal relationship between the media and the medical profession was summed up in its evidence to a 1960s committee on broadcasting: 'nothing but good can come from the acceptance of the idea, encouraged by *good* medical broadcasts, that the doctor has a scientific and logical basis for his actions, and does his best to carry them out with compassion for the sick and suffering.' (Quoted by Karpf, p. 5, emphasis added.)

Yet despite these concerns by the profession about the tendency of the media to misrepresent medicine: 'the medical establishment generally wants the media to reproduce medical values and ideology.' (p. 5)

From what has been said so far about Karpf's approach, you may wonder what this has to do with social psychology or with the domain of Book 3 (*Identities, Groups and Social Issues*). Karpf's way of looking at the relationship between media professionals and medical professionals, the implications this nexus has for media coverage, and the impact the resultant social representations have on the public, are all relevant to the way in which Book 3 analyses the sociocultural domain. For a start, Karpf is at pains to take seriously the contradictions and complexities that characterize the web of connections linking the media, the medical profession and the government: 'Programmes are produced by real people who aren't simply the victims of false consciousness or institutional lackeys who suspend all critical impulses for promotion's sake. They do exercise an autonomy of sorts, though within limits.' (p. 7)

The book rejects the idea that all medical programmes are inevitably uncritical of medicine. It also resists the temptation to see media representations of medicine as a problem located either in the media or in medicine. Each of these strategies, says Karpf, assumes that there is an unproblematic and scientific thing called medicine, which the media should reflect or convey. So what is the task for those wanting to make sense of the role of the media in creating and disseminating social representations of medicine?

According to Karpf, to understand the way in which information about medicine is presented by the media we must go beyond thinking about questions of distortion and bias. This means giving up the idea 'that the medical profession's view of medicine is necessarily and invariably the only authentic one, and treat its definitions instead as only one among a number of other, competing accounts of medical practice.' (p. 8)

This shift in perspective (away from the idea of absolute truths, of biased reporters, of all-powerful doctors) opens the way to asking questions about the different approaches to medicine in the media, about the particular images which dominate at certain times and why media representations change.

Using this frame of reference, Karpf's book reviews a number of different themes, starting with the way in which television and radio programmes dealing with health and medicine are structured. Her chapter 'Health talk' takes us back to the early days of broadcasting and creates a sense of *déjà vu*. Her investigation finds that in the 1920s, 1930s and 1940s, the media were promoting fitness and healthy eating. Early radio talks about health in 1927 attracted an audience of 10 million and generated 20,000 letters in three months. Karpf makes the point that in the early days of broadcasting, the BBC was preoccupied with health rather than medicine. She suggests that the main reason for the media's obsession with health lay in the economic conditions of the time. Austerity gave rise to 'a punitive individualism where each citizen had a moral duty to make themselves fit'.

In the early days of the NHS, there was very little public debate about deficiencies in the healthcare system. But by the late 1970s, consumer critiques of health had become commonplace. In a section entitled *The Birth of the Patient*, Karpf seeks to explain why users of the health service started to get a hearing on television. She attributes this to a shift in public discourse which started in the 1960s, and which moved talk away from production as the site of struggle to consumption as the contested sphere, to the fact that:

> The old 'workerist' notions — that the only valid struggles took place in the factory or down the mine — were edged out by the new interest in the community and the home: you could be just as oppressed in the privacy of your own bedroom, school or GP's surgery. The language of social class and centralized, industrial struggle gave way to local and community organization. And in public debate, consumerism was the new ideology: in the 1960s we were all reconstituted as consumers.
>
> (p. 57)

Did this shift in emphasis lead to a diminution in the power of medical experts? According to Karpf, the social authority of medicine remains intact despite massive social changes. Medicine, she claims, has redrawn the boundaries of what it can do. Paradoxically, it is quite often doctors who talk about how individuals can look after themselves. And it is still the doctor who lends legitimacy to the new health regimes. The new emphasis on health has created new jobs in health promotion for those who are medically trained.

But although, on the surface, the type of *discourse* presented on television and radio appears to have diversified to include a consumer approach and a look-after-yourself approach, alongside the medical approach, all three approaches share similar premises. They all emphasize illness as individually experienced and caused, and play down its economic and environmental origins. And all three, to a greater or lesser extent, defer to medical definitions of health and illness.

What Karpf argues throughout her study is that the relationship between media portrayals of medicine and audience response is much more complex than early investigators had imagined. In the early days of mass media research, the audience was seen as passive recipients of the media message. Today it is widely recognized that the audience, by sophisticatedly discounting and counter-arguing with what they see, hear or read, is an active participant in the production of the media message. Does this mean then that we can discount the impact of the media in creating or disseminating ideas about medicine, health and illness? Karpf does not come to this conclusion. Instead, she maintains that 'health and medical programming plays a significant role in shaping public debate and the climate of opinion, both in what it chooses to address and what it doesn't, through its "symbolic crusades" and moral panics, its sudden creation of social problems, its ongoing obsessions and its routine omissions.' (p. 230)

The media in our society has an agenda-setting role. Although it may not be influential in terms of telling people *what* to think, it is successful in telling audiences what to think *about*.

Karpf concludes that the media 'play a major role in establishing the salience of different issues in public debate, of defining which aspects are important and which aren't, the terms in which they're discussed and who discusses them.' (p. 230)

None of what has been said about the role of the media in setting a health agenda should be taken to mean that audiences uncritically swallow these messages. As we saw when we looked at Cornwell's study, people are quite capable of producing varying accounts (what she termed public and private accounts) of health and illness. Karpf acknowledges that viewers and listeners probably hold contradictory views on health and medicine, simultaneously expressing public or official accounts and private or unofficial ones.

When the BBC interviewed 1,000 adults on their attitudes towards health, these contradictions were strikingly displayed. The vast majority — 92 per cent — agreed with the statement that 'staying healthy is an individual's responsibility' (what might be termed the 'official' or 'public view'). At the same time, when asked to rank the most serious health risks (from a list) in order of importance, nuclear waste and pollution emerged as second and third after smoking, with dietary factors like too much fat and too much sugar much lower down the scale (and after stress).

(p. 30)

How did the BBC interpret these findings? According to Karpf, instead of taking this as an indication of the coexistence of contradictory beliefs, the investigators judged it to be a sign of public confusion. Karpf's ideas and her approach will prepare you for the way Book 3 authors deal with the anomalies and ambiguities of social life.

3.4   Tensions and conflicts in healthcare systems: gender relations

At various points in the Trigger Unit, we have touched on the fact that there are recurrent tensions in health care that go beyond the relationship of individual patients and clinicians. Some of these arise through technological developments. For instance, when we looked at individual accounts of illness, we heard how the 'high tech' medicine associated with intensive care can result in patients feeling dehumanized. Some tensions have to do with the coexistence of public and private views. Thus, when we examined Cornwell's study we saw how people have conflicting and often ambivalent expectations about GPs and other healthcare professionals. In the same section, we saw that patients and doctors do not always share the same agenda. Consequently, patients often find it difficult to communicate with doctors and frequently come away from consultations feeling that they have not had a chance to raise matters of concern. And in looking at medical socialization we saw how students experience inner conflicts as they struggle to acquire a professional identity. What we did not do, in any systematic way, however, was to question whether our social status and roles (e.g. male/female, parent, child, young/old, middle class/working class, black/Asian/white) have an impact on our health and our experiences of the healthcare system.

In keeping with the overarching theme of Book 3, this section will seek to relate these conflicts and tensions experienced at an individual level to social roles set within the wider sociocultural domain. We will consider whether the socially constructed divisions of labour and professional power struggles have a bearing on the way in which health care is organized and how groups and individuals experience the healthcare system. We will enquire about some of the dissatisfactions that have been expressed concerning health care, focusing on feminist critiques of the way in which doctors treat female patients. Finally, we shall see how the nursing profession, in an effort to redefine its role, is developing a new way of talking about nursing and about patient care.

To achieve this will require some consideration of the way in which history, culture and society impinge upon the psychology and experience of the individual. Posing such questions leads us to what is sometimes called a *sociological social psychology.*

In order to try to tease out the relationship between cultural practices, social institutions, professional groups and personal experience we will focus on two topics:

- women's experiences as users of healthcare services
- efforts to redefine the role of the nurse.

ACTIVITY 3.9   See if you can anticipate some of the charges which feminists have made against medicine as a social institution.

Check whether any items in your Resource File relate to this issue.

Women's experiences as users of healthcare services

In early studies of doctor–patient relationships, the gender of the two participants was virtually ignored. The assumption was that gender did not influence the interaction between the doctor and the patient.

> ... researchers may have accepted the convention of the western medical profession that doctors are somewhat 'sexless' and 'genderless' beings, and therefore that patients could talk to them, undress in front of them and be examined by them in an 'asexual' way. Little attempt was made to discover whether patients in reality perceived doctors in this way.

> (Miles, 1991, p. 154)

Incidentally, the same assumption was made about social class, race and ethnicity. It was thought that doctors treat all patients alike. Have you collected any material for your Resource File which suggests that experience of health care is influenced by group membership?

Over the last twenty years, there has been a considerable amount of research carried out to determine the ways in which gender is likely to shape medical consultations. You may well have views on the matter but before you proceed, test your beliefs by answering the following quiz questions.

Read through the following statements and tick those which you think are
true.

❑ In most western countries, women go to doctors more frequently than do men.

❑ Doctors see women patients as 'more trouble' than men.

❑ Patients with organic, physical and treatable diseases are considered less trouble than those with emotional and psychiatric problems and those with chronic diseases.

❑ Women present fewer emotional and psychiatric problems to GPs than do men.

❑ Female doctors are less aware of gender issues than their male counterparts.

❑ Female medical students are less sympathetic to feminist views than male doctors.

❑ Male doctors spend more time with patients than do female doctors.

❑ Doctors, in general, think that women are likely to make excessive demands on their time.

❑ Doctors are more likely to attribute psychological causes to the illnesses of female patients than male patients.

❑ Female patients receive fewer prescriptions for tranquillizers than do male patients.

Feedback is given in the 'Feedback for Activities' section on page 108 of this unit.

Research findings

In most western countries, women go to doctors more frequently than do men. (Miles, p. 63). There is also consistent evidence to show that doctors do *not* think about or treat their patients in an objective, uniform way. In his postal survey, Stimson (1976) found that the 453 GPs (gender undistinguished) he surveyed tended to regard women patients as more 'trouble' than men. This linked to their perception that patients with organic, physical and treatable diseases were less trouble than those who complained of emotional and psychiatric problems and those with chronic diseases. (And women are more apt to bring up emotional and psychiatric problems than men.)

Do male and female doctors differ in their attitudes towards female patients? It is difficult to answer this question because in much of the research the doctors studied were males. However, there are indications that 'female doctors have different values and therefore see their women patients' roles in a different light from their male colleagues' (Miles, p. 155).

Miles goes on to suggest that:

> ... women doctors are likely to have different political and ideological views than male doctors concerning the position of women in society not only because they share the socialization and other experiences of women in general, but also because they themselves have broken out of the traditional pattern of women's lives by becoming doctors. *Their assumptions about women's place and roles and about the nature of women are thus likely to differ markedly from those of male doctors.*
>
> (p. 155, emphasis added)

There is also evidence that female doctors spend more time with patients than do male doctors.

If Miles is right in her interpretation of the research, then given the rising numbers of women entering medicine, are women likely to find doctors becoming more sympathetic to their concerns? Have you found differences between male and female doctors?

If we ignore the gender of the doctor, and ask whether there are consistent differences in the *treatment* meted out to male and female patients, it is hard to draw conclusions from the research. Some researchers (e.g. Lennane and Lennane, 1973) found that doctors systematically dismiss or minimize certain female complaints. They took this as evidence of sex bias on the part of doctors who did not take women's pains seriously. Other research concurs with the claim that doctors are prone to attribute women's complaints to psychological problems. However, as Miles points out, not *all* research has observed gender bias.

In recent years sociologists, such as Lesley Doyal (1994), have raised somewhat different issues about women's experiences of health care. One of her concerns is that male bias in both research and clinical decision making may lead to inappropriate diagnosis and treatment of women. She cites American and Australian research which shows that women are often omitted as subjects in medical research. At the same time, Doyal warns against simplistic critiques of medicine.

> Some of the earlier feminist critiques can now be seen as 'over-determined' in their negative assessment of the benefits some medical techniques can offer women, in their exaggeration of the power of individual doctors and in their assumption of the universality of unremitting sexism among all practitioners. There has also been a tendency on the part of some of these commentators to operate with a conspiracy model of 'nasty' doctors. Instead, we need a more interactive understanding of the relationship between women and their doctors, and an emphasis on the impact of the medical actions rather than the intentions of individual doctors.
>
> (p.146)

From this brief look at a very large literature, what conclusions can we draw about gender and health care? It is clear that doctors, as a group, have expectations about women as a social group and that this has a bearing on the conduct of clinical consultations. This is not to say that male doctors are inevitably sexist or that they treat all female patients in an identical manner. Doctors acquire meanings and values from the wider society as well as from the more restricted world of medicine. As debates relating to gender are brought into the public arena, doctors are likely to become more aware of the way in which their words and other actions are perceived by their female patients. And the rising number of female doctors should help to shift professional attitudes.

Efforts to redefine the role of the nurse

In looking at the sociocultural domain, one of the questions which is bound to arise is *why* is the social world organized in the way it is? For instance, why, until quite recently, has medicine been dominated by men, while nursing has been an all-female profession? Is this 'natural', reflecting the different natures, interests and capacities of the two sexes, or are there other reasons why this division of labour has arisen? And looking at the skills and training of the two professions, how has it happened that certain tasks have been defined as the sole responsibility of one group e.g. only doctors have been allowed to operate or to prescribe medicine, or to take blood, whereas nurses are expected to offer day-to-day bedside care and to work under the supervision of doctors? This section looks at the way in which seemingly permanent features of our social institutions are socially constructed and the process by which one group may seek to challenge the power of another by seeking to renegotiate its role.

Explaining gender differences   ACTIVITY 3.11

How would you explain the fact that, until recently, medicine was a predominantly male profession and that few men entered nursing? Do you think that there is one reason or multiple causes?

There are clear grounds for challenging the idea that men are somehow better suited to be doctors than women or that women make better nurses. (Not least the fact that the ratios are now changing: in medical schools, women now make up 50 per cent of the intake.) The explanation for the traditional gender divisions in our healthcare system is much more likely to reside in historical power imbalances between men and women which have both *limited* women's access to medicine and *discouraged* them from applying to medical school. Likewise, social pressures, together with low pay, have deterred men from entering nursing. The rest of this section will concentrate on recent efforts to change the role of nurses and the challenge this poses to the dominance of the medical profession.

Nurses and midwives make up almost half the total workforce of the health service. (And nine out of ten nurses are women.) By contrast, the proportion of doctors (and dentists) is small — just over 5 per cent of hospital staff, and another 5 per cent in family practitioner services (Pascall and Robinson, 1993, p. 85). When the Briggs Committee (1972) looked at nursing and midwifery, it claimed that the inherited images of these professions, dating back to the nineteenth century, still exerted a powerful impact. The committee's report suggested that doctors and nurses are viewed not as partners but as people in charge on the one hand (i.e. doctors) and their 'handmaidens' (i.e. nurses) on the other: 'In the process of providing care the doctor needed a skilled helper, and in the inherited image (still treasured by some) the nurse figures as such — a person who is strictly ancillary' (Briggs Committee, 1972, p. 255).

Much has happened in the NHS since 1972 but this notion that nurses are an ancillary, subservient group persists. Recruitment, training and pay all contribute to the hierarchical relationship between the two groups, but might gender also be implicated? John Albarran, a clinical tutor, thinks this is the case: 'Nursing is often seen as an extension of women's work and the nurturing role and therefore nurses are expected to be caring, unselfish and accepting of their less privileged position. This is further reinforced by the paternalistic medical model of care in which nurses have been assigned a subservient position which has made them internalize a passive role' (Albarron, 1995, p. 461).

Margaret Stacey (1991), a sociologist of health with a particular interest in questions of work and gender, has gathered evidence to show that male occupations have been more successful than female occupations in gaining work autonomy. But *why* have female-dominated occupations, such as nursing, been accorded lower status and lower pay than male-dominated domains of work? Witz (1994) cautions against simply blaming the medical profession for placing constrains on nurses' aspirations. She maintains that we need to place nursing in a broader *organizational and political context*. In the mid-1990s, major changes are taking place in nursing which could result in a challenge by nurses to the traditional

---

BOX 3.2 The new nursing

Nurses in the 1990s are in the process of putting into place a far-reaching occupational strategy which involves a redefinition of their role. Key elements include:

- the reform of nurse education (*Project 2000*), resulting in occupational control over what is taught and where it is taught

- a new focus on the content of nursing work, with calls for more autonomy and the emergence of a new *discourse of caring* in nursing (Witz, p. 24).

Of these two developments, practitioner autonomy (relating to the content of nursing), along with its associated way of talking about nursing, is the one which most directly challenges the traditional doctor-led model of health care.

---

hegemony of doctors over both nurses and patients. Political, demographic and economic changes may pave the way to nurses establishing a distinct sphere of competence within the healthcare division of labour.

According to Witz, the 'new nursing' is very much about demarcation and power relations between different occupational groups in the health division of labour (most notably doctors and nurses). How do the reformers in a profession go about making such changes? How do they go about winning the hearts and minds of the entire profession? How do they woo allies in other professions, get their message across to the public, persuade political groups, and cope with detractors? A campaign of this type requires rhetorical skill, because the main weapon for those advocating change is words. In Book 3, Chapter 3 you will learn about a new development in social psychology called *discursive psychology* which looks at 'what people do with their talk or writing'. This approach offers a fresh way of analysing public debate.

Reading the professional journals provides evidence that nurses are seeking to construct a new vision of the nursing role. Writing in the *Health Service Journal,* Christine Hancock, the General Secretary of the Royal College of Nurses, makes a very strong case for the inherent skills of nurses:

> With nurses delivering some 80 per cent of direct patient care, and given that a nurse is so often the patient's first and last point of contact with the health service, the value of a nurse on the board of every new purchasing health authority … is obvious.
>
> Some have stressed the value of nursing in ensuring the very highest standards of patient care. Others have praised nursing's cost-effectiveness at every level. Still more have said simply *that when it comes to understanding patient needs, nurses are the front-runners in the healthcare team.*
>
> *(1995, p. 23, emphasis added)*

Implicit in these statements is a rebuttal of the idea that the nurse is the doctor's 'handmaiden'. How are doctors responding to nurses' efforts to stake out a new professional identity? Having so long been the dominant profession, doctors must find it hard to grasp what is happening in nursing. At the time of preparing this unit, it is not clear how doctors will relate to these changes: 'the extent to which doctors will be willing to exchange their traditional "handmaidens" for true clinical partners, or even substitutes, is one of the most important questions posed by the new nursing.' (Witz, 1994, p. 33)

There are some indications that doctors are not happy with the idea that nurses in future will be 'actively involved in and trusted with patient care, not merely supervising its delivery on terms dictated by medicine' (Witz, 1994, p. 29). For example, one doctor expressed fears that the changes being proposed could end up with the doctor being relegated to

4 Conclusion: dealing with diversity

The purpose of the Trigger Unit has been to give you a preview of the way in which D317 is structured and to encourage you to be an active learner. Our topic matter, health and illness, has served as a jumping-off point for alerting you to some of the key features of the course and to signalling your role as a student of D317.

One of the significant features of the course is that it portrays social psychology as a complex, evolving discipline. At the heart of the course is the tension which results from the fact that social psychology is not a unitary field of study; it embraces *different* perspectives, crosses *different* domains and draws upon *different* research methods. But while diversity makes for a very rich and exciting discipline, we know that it can seem daunting to students who are anxious to know whether they have understood the story and taken away the intended messages. Tensions are bound to come about as you seek to integrate what you have learned and to test out your grasp of the perspectives and the type of knowledge each perspective constructs.

We have already mentioned that the course includes a fourth book, *Issues for Social Psychology*. This will be where problems relating to diversity will be addressed. The question of how (and whether) one unifies the various perspectives, the different conceptions of what it means to *do* social psychology, will be taken up by different authors. You will be provided with guidance in the Study Guides as to when to read particular chapters in *Issues for Social Psychology*. (You may wish to scan the table of contents at this point to have an overview of the book's coverage.) And the other books in this course will each confront the issue of diversity.

To return to your role as a student, it was suggested at the outset of this unit that a course which does not present its subject matter as an integrated, finished product makes special demands on its students. In particular, it demands critical thinking and a willingness to challenge what you have read. What we hope you will take forward to the rest of the course after reading the Trigger Unit will be a readiness to think things through for yourself, and to relate what you read in the course to your own life experiences. The Trigger Unit has been built around activities and we hope that you will continue to be an active learner throughout the rest of the course.

Feedback for activities

Activity 1

How we experience the three domains: some examples

The individual, personal domain is likely to overshadow the other two when an individual is seriously ill. Horizons are liable to shrink when the person is pre-occupied with getting better or surviving. Likewise, at times of personal crises, an individual may be disinterested in what is happening in the outside world.

Interpersonal events may seem to dominate one's life if one is involved in a very powerful relationship. When people fall in love they may be so con-cerned about what is happening between them and their partner that the other domains temporarily recede. The intensity of the relationship may be such that one loses one's self and severs contact with wider social networks. Similarly, many mothers go through a period when they find themselves totally absorbed in their relationship with their newborn baby. Ironically, very negative, hostile relationships may have the same effect. Individuals who become locked into a power struggle may show signs of being fixated on the interpersonal domain.

The sociocultural domain may loom large at times of social change or crisis. For example, when an individual moves country, a large part of their effort and attention will be directed towards trying to comprehend and master the new environment. Not only will there be language barriers to overcome, but all of the taken-for-granted meanings of social life will suddenly need to be thought about. Similarly, changing job may result in a period of readjustment in which the individual has to learn a new organizational culture.

Activity 2.1

Caring relationships — some examples

Personal, informal relations

- parents providing day-to-day care for a young child

- adults caring for their aged parent(s)

- wife providing care to husband (laundry, cooking, cleaning)

- older child caring for a younger sibling (e.g. taking child to school, getting them ready for bed)

- grandchild carrying out errands for grandparents

- one neighbour providing help for another neighbour

- voluntary work through a church or charity e.g. visiting individuals who are house-bound

Formal, paid, professional relations

- health visitor providing advice and support to a new mother
- social worker supporting a troubled teenager
- home help cleaning someone's flat
- GP looking after someone who is terminally ill
- care assistant looking after a handicapped adolescent

Activity 2.2

The construction of research topics

Feminists suggest that the main reason why unpaid, informal caring was so long ignored by researchers and policy makers is that it tends to be carried out by women at home and was seen as a 'natural' part of women's role. Writers such as Ann Oakley maintain that the social sciences reproduced the sexist attitudes of the wider society. Hence, what was deemed important was what went on in the 'real' world, outside the domestic sphere. So, because caring tends to be invisible and carried out by women, it was not defined as 'work' and was not researched.

Why the recent interest in caring?

- Feminists researchers have deemed this to be a legitimate and important topic.
- Demographic changes (a fall in the birth rate and an increase in life expectancy) have alerted policy analysts and politicians to the need to understand what is involved in providing care.
- An increase in the numbers of women in full-time employment means that we can no longer assume that women are available to provide informal care.
- Family changes (rises in divorce rates, increased geographical mobility) mean that it is often difficult for people to provide care to other family members.
- The development of a commercial market in care (e.g. private residential nursing homes, private agencies providing care assistants, private day care for children) has meant that there is interest in understanding what caring entails in order to be able to cost it. Insurance companies are aware of the need to be able to put a financial figure to care because of the need to arrive at estimates as to what it would cost, for example, to provide a replacement for a mother who is seriously ill for four or five months. The same consideration arises in court cases where damages are sought to cover the case of caring following an accident which results in the individual being permanently handicapped.

- A commitment to 'community care' has put care high on the political agenda. The government, at present, is seeking ways to enable people who need care to be cared for outside institutions. Health services and social services are seeking to define 'packages of care'; this is likely to provide further incentives for studying both formal and informal care.

Activity 2.6

Generalizing about clinical consultations

What needs to be taken into account in setting up a study and analysing the results (comparing one practice with another)? Here is an attempt to map out the different types of variables which would need to be taken into consideration.

- *The nature of the population of patients registered with the GP*: e.g. how many patients are registered; the age/sex mix of the patients; the social class mix of the patient population; the turnover in the register (i.e. how stable is the population?); ethnicity; whether it is an urban or a rural practice.

- *Factors relating to the doctors:* e.g. number of partners in the practice; length of time the doctor(s) has been in the practice; age and sex of the partners; their training in the use of the computer system; general familiarity with computers; length of time the computer has been in use; enthusiasm and confidence of the users; where and when the doctors trained in medicine.

- *Factors relating to the consulting room*: e.g. size and layout of the room; where the computer is located; where the patient and the doctor are seated.

- *Factors relating to the observed consultations*: e.g. the reason for the encounter (routine, crisis); the history of the relationship between the patient and the GP (e.g. how well the doctor knows the patient); whether the patient has a chronic condition (asthma, arthritis, diabetes).

Activity 2.7

Sociocultural factors shaping public expectations

As the concept of patients' rights becomes commonplace (e.g. the Patients' Charter) patients are becoming more assertive ('demanding'). Compared to the immediate post-war population, patients today see medicine more as a right than something for which they should feel thankful. Patients are not so in awe of doctors; they see themselves as the doctor's equal. Patients are starting to think of themselves as consumers ('we're paying for this').

Increased media coverage (news, popular dramas, documentaries) of medical matters may result in a more informed population. Conversely, it may raise expectations about what the doctor should be able to provide. The media also provide viewers with a more critical approach to medicine and the NHS, such as publicity surrounding malpractice suits and legal action against doctors and hospitals. The net result is that the public is more aware of the fallibility of doctors and of the fact that there is not always consensus on how to treat patients. At the same time, patients hear about experimental treatments and may expect them to be immediately available.

The impact of the women's movement in stimulating debate about women's health and how doctors treat women has created an environment in which it has become easier for women to question or challenge medical experts.

Growing awareness of 'alternative medicine' and increasing interest in complementary medicine has made the public suspicious or doubtful about the efficacy of high technology medicine or the so-called 'biomedical model'.

A more educated, better informed public has new expectations of healthcare professionals.

Activity 2.21

Negotiating with healthcare professionals

1   Influencing factors

- social status of the two parties

- resources of the two (intellectual, social and fiscal)

- familiarity of each party with his or her role

- who does the asking and who has the power to refuse

- the site and physical arrangements for the negotiations

- fiscal outcomes contingent on the negotiation process

- availability of third parties to arbitrate

- answerability of each party to independent constituencies

- nature of the problem, request and goals

- the ideologies or perspectives available to the two parties and whether they are compatible

- options available to the two parties

2   Relevance to patient–professional relationships

I feel that all of these factors have a bearing on the way in which patients negotiate with healthcare professionals.

3   Balance of power

Most patients feel that there is an unequal relationship between themselves and professionals. This is not to say that patients are powerless. However, doctors, and to a lesser degree other professionals, are the ones with the expert training; they are experienced by patients as more powerful in that they decide what examinations to carry out, what diagnosis to make, whether to refer the patient and whether to prescribe a drug. What power does the patient have? The patient may withdraw from the consultation, refuse to comply with the prescribed treatment, seek a second opinion, change his or her GP or seek some form of alternative treatment. As a last resort, the patient may make a complaint or seek legal redress.

Activity 2.22

Estimate the number of carers

A 1985 General Household Survey Report on informal carers quoted by Green (1988) yielded the following information.

In Great Britain, in 1985, 6 million people over the age of 16 years were informal carers for a mentally or physically disabled or elderly person. This equates to 1 adult in 7, or 14 per cent of the population. 1 in 5 households contained a carer. Of the total population of carers, 3.5 million were women and 2.5 million were men.

The vast majority of dependent people (irrespective of the nature of their dependency) live in the community and the main responsibility for their care rests with informal, unpaid carers.

Activity 2.27

Generalizing to other cultures

The aim of this feedback is *not* to provide answers to the questions posed, but to get you to think about culture, social stereotypes and social expectations. In the absence of empirical studies on the way in which culture shapes expectations regarding kinship responsibilities, these comments must be seen as tentative hypotheses. There is little doubt that traditional, non-urban cultures have placed great emphasis on the role of the family in caring for kin. A corollary of this has been the expectation that the desires and ambitions of the individual may need to be subjugated to the interests of the family. In traditional cultures, the expectation is that women are the care givers and that, after childhood, children have a life-long responsibility to their family. Finally, these cultural values are often reinforced by religious beliefs.

There are two ways of interpreting this relationship between self and kin. On the one hand, cultures which make these sorts of demands on their members provide invaluable psychological and material support to individuals in times of crisis. On the other hand, for those who are obligated or expected to care, the burden can be very high.

Thinking about the questions posed in the text, what also needs to be remembered is that very often first or second generation immigrant groups experience a clash between their cultural values and the demands of their new environment. Changing social conditions (e.g. smaller houses, greater physical distance between family members) may make it difficult to maintain strong social support networks. In addition, apart from Jewish and Irish communities which have been here for many decades, for many communities which have only recently established roots, the problems associated with an ageing population are only now being faced. Hence, it is not possible to provide a definitive answer to the questions.

Activity 3.1

The influence of social and cultural factors on health and illness

Culture helps to set the agenda by creating expectations, e.g. what do we expect from our bodies? What do we expect from healthcare professionals? What is the correct or proper response to illness? Also, the way in which health care is organised and managed largely determines how (and whether) we have access to services. What follows are some specific illustrations of these points.

- The society in which we live determines our access to health care (e.g. how professionals are organized and regulated; the way in which health care is financed).

- Social class affects access to resources which make for a healthy or unhealthy life-style.

- The economic and industrial base of the society influences the environment, which in turn has an impact on health.

- How healthcare professionals are recruited, trained and organized affects the way in which they see their role and how they interact with the public.

- The mass media create and disseminate ideas about health and illness.

- Cultural practices and rituals define and give shape to biological events such as pregnancy, birth, adolescence, illness, ageing, death/dying, disfigurement, disease and disability.

- Our place in society (e.g. gender, race) affects the way in which we are socialized and the expectations we develop about our bodies and about health and illness.

- Technological developments have an impact on health and illness: both within medicine, and within society.

Activity 3.2

Why do individuals study medicine or nursing?

At their initial interview, medical students are usually asked to provide some explanation as to *why* they want to study medicine. Quite often the interview panel is seeking to establish what the candidate knows about medicine as a profession and how realistic he or she is about what is involved in being a doctor.

Here are some of the points students make in reply:

- a desire to help people

- an interest in science and research

- excitement with the way in which scientific discoveries can relieve pain and/or improve the quality of life

- medicine provides an opportunity to use science to help people

- enormous job satisfaction from this career

- family tradition (father, mother, grandfather, etc. are doctors)

- very varied and interesting work

- opportunities for travel.

Broadly speaking, these responses can be classed in terms of two different sets of motives:

- altruistic responses (the opportunity to help people and to combat disease)

- the challenge of doing clinical research (e.g. finding a cure for AIDS or for cancer).

These are not mutually exclusive; both are frequently mentioned by the same candidate, but candidates tend to give priority to one or the other in their verbal responses. Mingled with the altruistic response one finds that many candidates are attracted by what they perceive to be the public image of doctors as good, caring, noble people.

Of course, these public responses are not the whole story. Candidates seeking entry to medical school may well have other motives, some of which they would be reluctant to mention. For example:

- perceived social prestige of medicine

- financial rewards

- parental pressures

- job security.

Finally, psychodynamic theorists would remind us that there may well be unconscious reasons for seeking a career as a doctor or in one of the other caring professions. It may be that individuals are attracted to medicine because it meets their own hidden needs or helps to resolve certain unconscious conflicts.

Activity 3.7

The social construction of medical knowledge

Arguments against the notion that medicine is 'a social product'

Medicine is based on science and is not a social product in the way that literature or the cinema clearly are. The methods of science are transcultural: findings and discoveries made in one culture can be applied in any other culture. (For example, antibiotics developed in the UK will work in the Far East or in South America.) Even if the doctor and the patient are from two different cultures, examination and treatment are still possible. This shows that medicine, rather than being culture-bound, is universal in its application.

Evidence and arguments to support the claim that medicine is 'a social product'

Experts now agree that only 15 per cent of clinical interventions are based on objective scientific evidence to show that they do more good than harm. This means that most of what doctors do in treating patients derives not from science but from their beliefs, where they happened to train, their social and professional networks, their prejudices, what conferences they happen to attend, and what journals they happen to read. Even in western societies, there are big differences between cultures (e.g. France versus Britain versus Germany) in the way doctors think about the human body and the forms of treatment patients receive. In her book, *Medicine and Culture*, Lynn Payer (1990) provides fascinating examples of the cultural biases in medicine. Medical anthropologists (e.g. Helman, 1990) have also provided evidence of the way in which culture permeates medical systems. He points to studies which show that variations in diagnosis and treatment between countries cannot be explained solely by disparities in the health of their populations. He concludes that it is the underlying cultural values of a society that play an important role in determining how ill-health is both diagnosed and then treated.

Activity 3.10

Quiz answers

In most western countries, women   *True* (Miles, 1991)
go to doctors more frequently than do men.

(There are various reasons for this, one having to do with biology. Pregnancy and gynaecological problems account for some of the differences in consultation rates. In addition, there is evidence that women are more willing than men to seek medical help. Finally, it has been suggested that women are in a better position to go to the doctor's surgery than are men.)

Doctors see women patients as 'more trouble' than men.	*True* (Stimson, 1976)
Patients with organic, physical and treatable diseases are considered less trouble than those with emotional and psychiatric problems and those with chronic diseases.	*True* (Stimson, 1976)
Women present fewer emotional and psychiatric problems to GPs than do men.	*False* (Briscoe, 1987)
Female doctors are less aware of gender issues than their male counterparts.	*False* (Heins et al., 1979; Leichner and Harper, 1982)
Female medical students are less sympathetic to feminist views than male doctors.	*False* (Lesserman, 1981)
Male doctors spend more time with patients than do female doctors.	*False* (Langwell, 1982)
Doctors in general think that women are likely to make excessive demands on their time.	*True* (Bernstein and Kane, 1981)
Doctors are more likely to attribute psychological causes to the illnesses of female patients than male patients.	*True* (Wallen et al., 1979)
Female patients receive fewer prescriptions for tranquillizers than do male patients.	*False* (Cooperstock, 1978)

References

Albarran, J.W. (1995) 'Should nurses be politically aware?', *British Journal of Nursing*, vol. 4, no 8, pp. 461–5.

Argyle, M. (1996) 'The experimental study of relationships', Reading C in Miell, D. and Dallos, R. (eds.).

Armstrong, D. (1989) *An Outline of Sociology as Applied to Medicine*, London, Wright.

Balint, E., Courtenay, M., Elder, A., Hull, S. and Julian, P. (1993) *The Doctor, the Patient and the Group: Balint Revisited*, London, Routledge.

Balint, M. (1964) *The Doctor, his Patient and the Illness*, London, Pitman.

Banister, P. et al. (1994) *Qualitative Methods in Psychology: A Research Guide*, Buckingham, Open University Press.

Baron, R.J. (1985) 'An introduction to medical phenomenology: I can't hear you while I'm listening', *Annals of Internal Medicine*, vol. 103, pp. 606–11.

Becker, H.S., Geer, B., Hughes, E.C. and Strauss, A.L. (1961) *Boys in White: Student Culture in Medical School,* Chicago, University of Chicago Press.

Bennett, G. (1987) *The Wound and the Doctor: Healing, Technology and Power in Modern Medicine,* London, Secker & Warburg.

Bernstein, B. and Kane, R. (1981) 'Physicians' attitudes toward female patients', *Medical Care,* vol. 19 (6), p. 600.

Bridgstock, G. *Me and My Health* articles in the *Evening Standard*:

> Diane Abbott, 22 February 1994, p. 42
>
> Jeff Banks, 12 April 1994, p. 41
>
> Max Bygraves, 23 April 1993, p. 43
>
> Jim Davidson, 11 January 1994, p. 35
>
> Maeve Haran, 23 August 1994, p. 27
>
> Virginia Ironside, 21 June 1994, p. 45
>
> Lynda La Plante, 16 July 1993, p. 43
>
> Claire Tomalin, 25 October 1994, p. 39
>
> Sir Peregrine Worsthorne, 24 May 1994, p. 26

Briggs Committee (1972) *Report of the Committee on Nursing,* Cmnd. 5115, London, HMSO; extract from Chapter 2 'Nurses, midwives and the public: images and realities. Report of the Briggs Committee on Nursing' in Black, N. et al. (eds.) (1984) *Health and Disease: A Reader,* Buckingham, Open University Press.

Briscoe, M. (1987) 'Why do people go to the doctor? Sex differences in the correlation of GP consultations', *Social Science and Medicine,* vol. 25, pp. 507–13.

Brody R (1987) *Stories of Sickness,* New Haven, Yale University Press.

Byrne, P.S. and Long, B.E. (1976) *Doctors Talking to Patients,* London, HMSO.

Cassell, E.J. (1985) *Talking with Patients, Volume 1, The Theory of Doctor–Patient Communication,* Cambridge; Mass., The MIT Press.

Cooperstock, R. (1978) 'Sex difference in psychotropic drug use', *Social Science and Medicine,* vol. 12, pp. 179–86.

Cornwell, J. (1984) *Hard-earned Lives: Accounts of Health and Illness from East London,* London, Tavistock.

Dallos, R. (1996) 'Change and transformations of relationships' in Miell, D. and Dallos, R. (eds.).

Daly, J., McDonald, I. and Willis, E. (eds.) (1992) *Researching Health Care: Designs, Dilemmas, Disciplines,* London, Routledge.

D'Souza, M. (1995) 'Professional differences', Letters page, *Student British Medical Journal,* vol. 3, p. 85 (March).

DHSS (1981) *Growing Old,* Cmnd. 8173, London, HMSO.

Donnelly, W.J. (1988) 'Righting the medical record: transforming chronicle into story', *Journal of the American Medical Association,* vol. 260, No. 6, pp. 823–5.

Doyal, L. (1994) 'Changing medicine? Gender and the politics of health care', in Gabe, J., Kelleher, D. and Williams, G. (eds.) (1994) *Challenging Medicine*, London, Routledge.

Dunnell, K. and Cartwright, A. (1972) *Medicine Takers, Prescribers and Hoarders*, London, Routledge and Kegan Paul.

Ehrenreich, B. and English, D. (1974) *Complaints and Disorders: The Sexual Politics of Sickness*, London, Compendium.

Eliott, B.J. (1994) 'A content analysis of the health information provision in women's weekly magazines', *Health Libraries Review*, vol. 11, pp. 96–103.

Fox, R.C. (1974) *Essays in Medical Sociology: Journey into the Field*, New York, Wiley.

Fox, R.C. (1974a) 'Training for uncertainty', in *Essays in Medical Sociology: Journey into the Field*, New York, Wiley.

Fox, R.C. (1974b) 'The autopsy: its place in the attitude-learning of second-year medical students' in *Essays in Medical Sociology: Journey into the Field*, New York, Wiley.

General Medical Council (1993) *Tomorrow's Doctors: Recommendations on Undergraduate Medical Education*, London, GMC.

Goffman, E. (1961) *Encounters: Two Studies in the Sociology of Interaction*, Indianapolis, Bobbs-Merrill.

Gore, S. (1989) 'Social networks and social supports in health care' in Freeman, H.E. and Levine, S. (eds.), *Handbook of Medical Sociology* (4th edition), Englewood Cliffs; NJ, Prentice Hall.

Green, H. (1988) *General Household Survey 1985: Informal Carers*, London, HMSO.

Hafferty, F.W. (1991) *Into the Valley: Death and the Socialization of Medical Students*, New Haven, Yale University Press.

Hancock, C. (1995) 'Nurses' right to be on board', *Health Services Journal*, vol. 105, p. 23 (May).

Harper, G. (1993) 'Breaking taboos and steadying the self in medical school', *The Lancet*, vol. 342, pp. 913–15.

Harris, M (1994) *Magic in the Surgery*, London, The Social Affairs Unit.

Heins, M., Hendricks, J. and Martindale, L. (1979) 'Attitudes of women and men physicians', *American Journal of Public Health*, vol. 69, pp. 132–9.

Helman, C.G. (1990) *Culture, Health and Illness: An Introduction for Health Professionals* (2nd edition) London, Wright.

Herzlich, C. (1973), *Health and Illness: A Social Psychological Analysis* (trans. by D. Graham), London, Academic Press.

Ichheiser, G. (1970) *Appearances and Realities: misunderstandings in human relations*, San Fransisco, Jossey-Bass.

Jones, A.D., Stewart, A. and Winter, D.G. (1974) 'Socialization and themes in popular drama: An analysis of the content of child-rearing manuals and Don Juan plays in sixteenth to twentieth centuries', *European Journal of Social Psychology*, vol. 4, (1), pp. 65–84.

Karpf, A. (1988), *Doctoring the Media: The Reporting of Health and Medicine*, London, Routledge.

Lalljee, M. (1996) 'The interpreting self: an experimentalist perspective' in Stevens, R. (ed,) (1996) *Understanding the Self*, London, Sage.

Langwell, K.M. (1982) 'Differences by sex in economic returns with physician specialization', *Journal of Health Politics, Policy and Law*, vol. 6, pp. 752–61.

Lazare, A., Eisenthal, S., Frank, A. and Stoeckle, J.D. (1978) 'Studies on a negotiated approach to patienthood' in Stoeckle J.D. (ed.) (1987) *Encounters Between Patients and Doctors*, Cambridge; Mass., The MIT Press.

Leichner, P. and Harper, D. (1982) 'Sex role ideology among physicians', *Canadian Medical Association Journal,* vol. 127, p. 380.

Lennane, J.K. and Lennane, R.J. (1973) 'Alleged psychogenic disorders in women – a possible manifestation of sexual prejudice', *New England Journal of Medicine,* vol. 288, 6.

Lesserman, J. (1981) *Men and Women in Medical School*, New York, Praeger.

Lowry, S. (1993) *Medical Education*, London, British Medical Journal Publishing Group.

Lupton, D. (1994) *Medicine as Culture: Illness, Disease and the Body in Western Societies,* London, Sage.

Mackey, M. (1995) 'Nurses are not doctors' enemies', Letters page of *Student British Medical Journal,* vol. 3, pp. 215–6.

Merton, R.K., Reader, G.G. and Kendell, P.L. (1957) *The Student-Physician: Introductory Studies in the Sociology of Medical Education,* Cambridge; Mass., Harvard University Press.

Miell, D. and Croghan, R. (1996) 'Examining the wider context of social relationships' in Miell, D. and Dallos, R. (eds.).

Miell, D. and Dallos, R. (eds.) (1996) *Social Interaction and Personal Relationships*, London, Sage/The Open University (Book 2 of the course).

Miles, A. (1991) *Women, Health and Medicine*, Buckingham, Open University Press.

Morgan, H. and Thomas, K. (1996) 'A psychodynamic perspective on group processes' in Wetherell, M. (ed.).

Moscovici, S. (1984) 'The phenomenon of social representations' in Farr, R.M. and Moscovi, S. (eds) *Social Representations*, Cambridge, Cambridge University Press.

Oakley, A. (1992) *Social Support and Motherhood: The Natural History of a Research Project*, Oxford, Blackwell.

Parker, G. (1989) *With Due Care and Attention: a Review of Research on Informal Care* (2nd edition), London, Family Policy Studies Centre.

Parker, G. (1993) *With this Body: Caring and Disability in Marriage*, Buckingham, Open University Press.

Parker, G. (1991) 'They've got their own lives to lead: carers and dependent people talking about family and neighbourhood help' in Hutton, J., Hutton, S., Pinch, T. and Shiell, A. (eds.) (1991) *Dependency to Enterprise*, London, Routledge.

Pascall, G. and Robinson, K. (1993) 'Health work: division in health-care labour' in Davey, B. and Popay, J. (eds.) (1993) *Dilemmas in Health Care*, Buckingham, Open University Press.

Payer, L. (1990) *Medicine and Culture: Notions of Health and Sickness,* London, Victor Gollancz.

Pendleton, D., Schofield, T., Tate, P. and Havelock, P. (1984), *The Consultation: An Approach to Learning and Teaching,* Oxford, Oxford University Press.

Potter, J. (1996) 'Attitudes, social representations and discursive psychology' in Wetherell, M. (ed.)

Radley, A. (ed.) (1993) 'Introduction' in *Worlds of Illness: Biographical and Cultural Perspectives on Health and Disease*, London, Routledge.

Radley, A. (1996) 'Relationships in detail: the study of social interaction' in Miell, D. and Dallos, R. (eds.).

Rogers W.S. (1991) *Explaining Health and Illness: An Exploration of Diversity,* London, Harvester.

Roter, D. (1979) 'Altering patient behaviour in interaction with providers' in Oborne, D.J., Gruneberg, M.M. and Eiser J.R. (eds.) (1979) *Research in Psychology and Medicine,* vol. 2, London, Academic Press.

Sacks, O. (1984) *A Leg to Stand On*, New York, Summit Books.

Sacks, O. (1985) *The Man who Mistook his Wife for a Hat*, London, Duckworth.

Spindler, S. (1992) *Doctors To Be,* London, BBC Books.

Stacey, M. (1991) *The Sociology of Health and Healing,* London, Routledge.

Stevens, R. (ed.) (1996) *Understanding the Self*, London, Sage/The Open University (Book 1 of the course).

Stevens, R. (1996) 'The reflexive self: an experiential perspective' in Stevens, R. (ed.).

Stimson, G. (1976) 'General practitioners, "trouble" and types of patient' in Stacey, M. (ed.) *The Sociology of the NHS Sociological Review Monographs,* No. 22, Keele, University of Keele.

Stimson, G.V. and Webb, B. (1975) *Going to See the Doctor: The Consultation Process in General Practice,* London, Routledge and Kegan Paul.

Szasz T.S. and Hollander, M.H. (1956) 'A contribution to the philosophy of medicine', *American Medical Association Archives of Internal Medicine*, XCVII, pp. 585–7.

Tamm, M.E. (1993), 'Models of health and disease', *British Journal of Medical Psychology,* vol. 66, pp. 213–28.

Taylor S. and Field, D. (1993) *Sociology of Health and Health Care*, Oxford, Blackwell.

Thomas, K. (1996) 'The defensive self: a psychodynamic perspective' in Stevens, R. (ed.).

Thomas, K. (1996) 'The psychodynamics of relating' in Miell, D. and Dallos, R. (eds.).

Thompson, J. (1984) 'Communicating with patients' in Fitzpatrick, R. et al. (eds.) (1984) *The Experience of Illness*, London, Tavistock.

Trevillion, S. (1992) *Caring in the Community: A Networking Approach to Community Partnership*, Harlow, Longman.

Viner, E.D. (1985) 'Life at the other end of the endotracheal tube: a physician's personal view of critical illness', *Progress in Critical Care Medicine*, vol. 2, pp. 3–13, Basel, Karger.

Wallen, J., Waitzkin, H. and Stoeckle, J.D. (1979) 'Physician stereotypes about female health and illness', *Women and Health*, vol. 4, pp. 135–46.

Watson, D (1996) 'Individuals and institutions' in Wetherell, M. (ed.).

Wetherell, M. (ed.) (1996) *Identities, Groups and Social Issues*, London, Sage/The Open University (Book 3 of the course).

Wetherell, M. (1996) 'Group conflict and the social psychology of racism' in Wetherell, M. (ed.).

Wetherell, M. and Maybin, J. (1996) 'The distributed self: a social constructionist perspective' in Stevens, R. (ed.).

Witz, A. (1994) 'The challenge of nursing' in Gabe, J., Kelleher, D. and Williams, G. (eds.) (1994) *Challenging Medicine*, London, Routledge.

Wolfenstein, M. (1951) 'The emergence of fun morality', *Journal of Social Issues*, vol. 7(4), pp. 15–25.

Zola, I. (1973) 'Pathways to the doctor: from person to patient', *Social Science and Medicine*, vol. 7, no 9, pp. 677–89.

Further Readings on Health Psychology

Broome, A.K. (ed.) (1989) *Health Psychology: Processes and Applications*, London, Chapman and Hall.

Gratchel, R.J., Baum, A. and Krantz, D.S. (1989) *An Introduction to Health Psychology*, New York, Random House.

Sheridan, C.L. and Radmacher, S.A. (1992) *Health Psychology: Challenging the Biomedical Model*, New York, John Wiley and Sons.

Me and my health: Diane Abbott

Source: 'Me and my health: Diane Abbott talks to Graham Bridgstock', *Evening Standard*, 22 February 1994, p. 42

The great thing about being 40 is you've more or less come to terms with yourself. I've started to go grey: perhaps being an MP caused it. But I never want to be 21 again, that's for sure. Then I longed to be like Twiggy. Now I know I'm never going to look like her.

Of course, I still wouldn't say no to being like one of those willowy Somalian ladies, tall and elegant and dark-skinned. But instead I'm short and dumpy and I have to live with it.

In fact, I'm 5ft 3in and I would rather not talk about my weight. Suffice to say I seem to have been on a diet all my life.

The trouble is I like all the things you shouldn't eat: butter, treacle tart, apple crumble, biscuits and cake, especially West Indian fruit-cake where the raisins and sultanas are steeped in dark rum for a couple of months.

No idea what I weighed at birth. All I know is I arrived at dawn a week early at St Mary's Hospital, Harrow Road. And I grew into a chubby little girl and always had my nose in a book. My mother reckoned I made my sight worse by reading under the bedclothes and I am extremely short-sighted, couldn't cope without my contact lenses.

She was a nurse and brought us up with a robust attitude to health: we were never allowed to stay home from school with just a sniff. At the time we thought we were being cheated. But I understand now and just work on regardless.

Their first child, a girl, was stillborn and father was always very attached to me. And he wouldn't allow us to be brought up in Jamaica, as was the custom with children born here then.

We had our tonsils out together when I was six and my brother Hugh was five. In those days they were whipped out automatically.

Otherwise the only time I've been in hospital was to have my son James Alexander Kojo — which is Ghanaian for born on a Monday — two years ago. Indeed, it was my first major encounter with the medical profession. Before that I hadn't been to a doctor for eight years.

When I became pregnant I registered with a husband-and-wife practice in Stoke Newington. It was an NHS birth at the Homerton Hospital in Hackney and I had the Queen's surgeon-gynaecologist Mr Marcus Setchell, who is a consultant there.

He has a wonderful bed-side manner: I didn't have a moment's worry throughout. My waters broke at 7.25 in the morning and the baby was born at 12.25 lunchtime which is pretty good for a woman of 38.

And it was an easy pregnancy. I swam a couple of days before, voted late in the House of Commons the week before and I was back at work within three weeks.

James weighed 7lb 8oz and has his father's features (Ghanaian-born architect David Thompson, 45; they are now in the throes of divorce) and my personality: he's very strong-willed, has a mind of his own.

Another one would be nice, yes: a girl would be company for James. Although I haven't a father in mind, I haven't ruled out marrying again either. If I'd started early I might have had lots of children.

When he was eight weeks I was reprimanded by the Serjeant at Arms for taking him through the division lobby in a sling. It was when we were voting on the Queen's Speech.

He was a great campaigner during the election, too, when he was only five months old. I'm sure a lot of people voted for him.

Just as well. I may have lost some votes through my fear of dogs. I was never bitten, but then I'm so timid the moment I hear barking and a dog throwing himself against a door I turn and leave.

At the moment I have a cold but it's only the cold everyone has. Healthwise I'm resilient, which is useful in politics. Mrs Thatcher is the same.

Hazards of the job? Well, it's hard to find time to exercise, though I work out occasionally in the Commons gym. But I would hate to be photographed in my leotard like the Princess of Wales. I would die if that happened to me.

It's difficult to stick to a sensible diet as well. Then there are the strange working hours — once I nodded off in the chamber but fortunately someone was kind enough to nudge me awake.

And there was a time when it seemed as though I hadn't slept for more than four hours a night for a year: James kept waking me.

He's grown out of that habit now. But when we were voting on Sunday trading I didn't get home until two in the morning (two-bedroom mews cottage in the heart of her Hackney North and Stoke Newington constituency) and had to be up again at six because that's when he wakes these days.

Yet somehow I manage to dream. Quite often I'm at the wheel of an out-of-control car in the rush hour. Obviously that's an anxiety dream because I can't drive anyway.

But never mind. I inherited a strong constitution. My forebears all come from sturdy peasant stock in Jamaica. My parents were both from Smithville, a little village up in the hills, a rural community who earn their living as smallholders. Just hens, vegetables and maybe a goat, which is killed and curried for special celebrations. It tastes like stringy mutton.

Like them I'd rather try to live a balanced life and not over-rely on medication. I don't take antibiotics or aspirins — it's rare for me to have a headache more than once in 12 months. So, although I take the baby regularly for check-ups, I seldom go to the doctor on my own account.

Long-lived parents? Father was a welder in a metal workshop, had a bronchial infection and died at the age of 54. However, he was a heavy smoker, 40 a day, and that's what killed him. My brother and I have never touched a cigarette.

Mother gave up nursing when she had us but went back after their divorce when I was 16 and worked in a mental hospital in Huddersfield until she retired.

Alas, she had quite a few problems. First kidney stones, then diabetes and finally, three years ago when she was 67, stomach cancer. It was diagnosed in March and she was gone by July.

That Easter I took her home to Jamaica for an emotional family reunion. She didn't want anybody to know she had cancer, felt it had some kind of stigma, so we had to pretend there was nothing wrong. Mind you, they were all well aware she had only a few weeks to live.

We stayed at my uncle Len's house and there were tears in his eyes when she said: 'See you next year!' And I had to turn away because I knew there would be tears in mine.

I'd like to end up like her mother Miss Di. I was named after her and she lived well into her seventies, had the sweetest disposition and was incredibly fit.

When we'd been on holiday in Jamaica and the time would come for us to say our farewells, she'd always insist on carrying our cases to the bus — on her head.

Me and my health: Jeff Banks

Source: 'Me and my health: Jeff Banks talks to Graham Bridgstock', *Evening Standard*, 12 April 1994, p. 41

My producer started kicking me. I was rolling around on the floor and he thought I was messing around. 'Stop sodding about. You're on in four minutes,' he said.

But I was in agony. I was about to present *The Clothes Show* from Olympia during London Fashion Week, two years ago, and I'd collapsed. 'Roger, I can't go on,' I said.'

Then someone noticed how white I was, called an ambulance and Selina Scott took over while I was whizzed off to Charing Cross Hospital in Hammersmith.

There they diagnosed the problem immediately: pancreatitis or inflammation of the pancreas.

I had no idea how serious it was. The following night I was due on television again for the British Fashion Awards from the Royal Albert Hall and I thought I would be out in time.

But the doctor said: 'No. Another hour and you'd have been dead. That is the gravity of it. So be thankful. You'll probably be in here three weeks.' And I was, though surgery was not necessary,

The most painful thing, otherwise, was a kick from a horse, last August, when I was out riding near our home in Cornwall. That tore all the ligaments on the out-side of my left leg and it was murder for four months.

A good patient, no. Demanding, though. I had a flat in Harley Street once, which is an ideal place to be sick and I was fine. And I have medicals for banks from time to time and the verdict is: 'Continue his overdraft. He's OK.'

A fortune-teller in India predicted I would live to 86. I was most disappointed and I'm determined to prove him wrong. I want to reach 100.

At 51, I certainly don't feel my age. I have all my own teeth and hair and still do the silly things I did when I was 25: clubbing, camping — I love the outdoors — and cycling.

In fact, I shall be off on the British Heart Foundation's 1994 London To Brighton Bike Ride for the second year, on 19 June.

I've never had heart trouble but I figure it's some kind of insurance. If anything ever did happen and I needed help, at least the British Heart Foundation would take my call.

'Well, we owe the bugger something,' they'd say.

Luckily, I had only one serious spill in my cycle-racing days. That was at Crystal Palace when I was 21 and brought my career on two wheels to a spectacular end.

I crashed, broke a collar bone and had all my kit stripped off but continued speeding along the track without my bike and totally naked. I limped away with only my badly scraped hands to preserve my modesty.

In the nip now I'm 11st 10lb and 5ft 8in. Ideally, I'd like to be 5ft 11in. Apart from that, I'm happy with my lot.

At birth — on St Patrick's Day — I was 7lb 13oz. That was at home, an end-of-terrace house in Drysiog Street, Ebbw Vale, with an outside lavatory and outside water.

You had to go out in the yard with a bucket or a jug and get it from a tap. And you bathed in an iron tub in front of an open fire in the back kitchen.

An only child, yes, and small and fast like a ferret. I played on the wing at football and fly-half at rugby.

The only health problem I had as a boy was a sinus infection, which they operated on when I was 15.

There were 10 of us in the ward. They had to remove the sinus sacks from above our eyes and everyone came to with a pair of lovely shiners. We looked like a row of pandas.

People say that's the reason for the nasal twang in my voice now. I could never be an opera singer, that's for sure.

Pisces, right. I'm gregarious, romantic, creative and I have a terrible temper, which surfaces occasionally.

When we had premises on the third floor in Mortimer Street, I threw a tray of coffee things out of the window — coffee, milk, sugar, cups, saucers, spoons, the lot — and they landed on the roof of a car. This guy got out and there was coffee running down his windscreen and broken china all around him.

Long-lived parents? They're both 79. Father left home when I was eight, came back when I was 16, left for three years when I was about 40, then came back again. Finally, a month before their 50th wedding anniversary, my mother left him. She felt she'd had enough.

These days she lives in Cornwall in a row of cottages overlooking the sea near our house and really enjoys life.

He has a retirement flat in Bromley and gave up cycling only a year ago. That was his life but he had no choice, he has glaucoma and his sight is impaired.

Regular exercise is vital for good health. So is the right food, and my breakfast is the same every day: orange juice, muesli with soya milk and herb tea. I never touch caffeine, the beastly stuff.

(A non-smoking, non-drinking vegetarian, he supplements this with Chlorella, a green Taiwanese algae pill which contains essential vitamins and minerals. It was developed for astronauts by the National Space Agency in America.)

On my travels I take my breakfast — and cheese and fruit bars — with me. You can't be too careful overseas, though I've visited 30 to 40 different countries and never been ill.

I sleep well too. We have a four-poster — seven feet square and 12 feet high — in Cornwall and a Louis XV bed in St John's Wood.

(The Banks family, not forgetting the basset hound Bisto and — at the last count — 24 hamsters, divide their time between the two properties.)

I don't wear pyjamas. People who do baffle me. No matter how cold it is, Eskimos and Chinese nomads always undress before getting into bed.

Normally, I average between five and six hours. I'm an early riser because I'm a Buddhist and have to be up to do my chanting.

Mental and physical health are absolutely entwined and I'm fortunate I can turn to that.

Buddhism sustained me during my divorce in 1981 (he has a daughter Grace, 22, from his first marriage to the 'Puppet on a String' singer Sandie Shaw) and when my business went bust about the same time.

Sandie was in a West End clinic recovering from an operation when I proposed. I can't remember the details except she had to sit on a rubber ring. That was on a Monday and we married on the Thursday.

When Grace was born I was away on business in Switzerland. However, I was present at St Mary's Hospital, Paddington, for the arrival of my daughters Coco, eight, and India, seven. They were both around the eight-pound mark.

Now my wife Sue says: 'Shall we try for a boy?' And I would quite like a son.

But then I think: 'By the time he's 15 he'll have a father with a bus pass.' And I am not sure that's such a bloody good idea.

Me and my health: Max Bygraves

Source: 'Me and my health: Max Bygraves talks to Graham Bridgstock', *Evening Standard*, 23 April 1993, p. 43

There were seven in the family but one died at birth. That left nine of us in a two-roomed council flat in Rotherhithe — two boys, four girls, Mum and Dad and my grandfather.

My brother Harry and I slept head-to-toe. The first time I ever spent a night in bed by myself was when I joined the RAF at 17. The next morning when I woke up and found myself alone I thought I was dead.

Friday night was bath night. But there was no bathroom and no hot water, just a galvanised iron tub in front of the fire.

You boiled the water in saucepans, then took turns. By the time mine came round, trying to find the face flannel was like looking for Geoff Love down a coalmine. Before bed we'd each have a dose of castor oil with half an orange to take away the taste.

But first my mother went through our hair with a fine-toothed comb, shaking everything back into the bath. Oh yes, we all had nits. The most serious thing I had as a kid, though, was impetigo.

The rent, when they got it, was eight shillings and four pence a week. The poverty was dreadful when I look back (as he does in *I Wanna Tell You A Funny Story*, Robson Books, £5.99). But we thought nothing of it. Everyone else around us was the same.

Besides, I got this wonderful routine out of it. You know the sort of thing: 'We couldn't even afford cutlery. We used to eat with our fingers. It took an hour and a half to finish a bowl of soup.'

Born at home, yes. I wanted to be near my mother. I was her second child. Harry was the first and the only one who didn't arrive on time. He turned up four months after they were married!

There was no such thing as the Pill then. The nearest thing to it was Beecham's Pills. The theory was: take six of those last thing at night and you're never in bed long enough for anything to happen.

They're all alive and well now except Harry and my sister Lily. They both died of cancer.

Mother was 84 when she went, which is not a bad innings, is it? Nothing wrong with her except old age. Altogether she had something like 43 children, grandchildren and great-grandchildren and she knew the names, addresses, birthdays and birth signs of them all.

Dad was 78, a former professional boxer and fit all his life till he became a heavy smoker. But he deteriorated fast in the end. That was cancer again.

Three of us were like Mother, three like Father. She was flaxen-haired, young-looking: I take after her. He was dark and went bald early.

They were both small, only 5ft 4in. Yet Harry was 6ft 1in. So am I. And all my sisters were pretty tall.

Since I left the RAF in 1945 I've put on only 12lb. Not bad for nearly 50 years. I was 12st 4lb then. Now I'm 13st 2lb.

That's not self-discipline. I'm lucky. I can eat anything. But if ever my body isn't functioning properly I switch to prunes and figs every morning for breakfast.

A fan put me on to the therapeutic value of grapes, too, and I always have some at home (flat in Westminster; house near Bournemouth with heated pool, basement gym and blue Rolls MB1 in the drive, and ranch-style property with 82 acres of parkland in Sydney, Australia, where he spends the winter). They're excellent for clearing the system and you can eat the whole fruit, skin, pips and all. But remember to wash them well.

I'm 70 now, but sometimes I don't feel any more than 45. I'm playing better golf than I've ever played, still have a 16 handicap. The only snag is I get a little weary round about the 14th and 18's a chore. They should cut it down, I think.

People say I look young. But then I've always had pretty good skin. That's my old grandad's recipe. Long before aftershave lotion he'd pour a spoonful of olive oil into a bottle of eau de cologne, shake it up, then pat it on his face or anywhere else where the skin was dry. And I've always done the same.

The doctor shakes his head in disbelief, reckons I'm as fit as a fiddle. 'You're a lucky man,' he says.

Only two problems lately. One was a virus I picked up which has made me partially deaf in one ear. It worried me actually because when I'm on stage I always work with the piano on that side. But the guy I saw about it said: 'Well, you still have quite a bit of hearing. It's just the balance that's gone.'

The other problem was a double hernia I had in Australia. I'd been overdoing the golf and singing too hard and finished up needing surgery, 19 stitches each side. The pain was excruciating, the worst I've ever known. But I can't complain. Got a wonderful routine out of that, too.

There I was sitting in a little room in the hospital when this nurse came in with a shaving brush, told me to take off all my clothes and put on a smock. Then she got down on her knees and shaved all round me ready for the operation.

'Would you like some tickets for my show?' I said.

'Who needs tickets?' she said.

All the ambulances were busy when I was ready to come home. So my wife Blossom hired a stretch limo and a chauffeur instead.

A good nurse? The best. Blos had me back on stage within a week. Mind you, I didn't enjoy it. I could hardly walk.

We've been married 50 years now. I was in the RAF when Anthony and Christine were born and on tour when Maxine arrived.

Like every other parent and grandparent, I worry about the family. Our grandson Michael died of legionnaires' disease when he was only 14, one of the first victims in this country and the youngest.

Not long after that I had a bout of shingles. Fortunately they got rid of it in 10 days or so with antibiotics. But work was the real cure.

Of course I don't need to work now. But then entertaining people, making them laugh, is my life. You can only read so much, play so much golf and sleep so much.

They asked Eric Sykes what he would like most of all. 'You really want to know?' he said. 'To be able to sleep like Max Bygraves.' And it's true. On the whole I average seven or eight hours undisturbed.

But once every couple of years I dream I'm in an aeroplane skimming over New York, weaving in and out of the skyscrapers, wondering if the pilot is going to make it with the wing-tips intact.

Then I wake up in a sweat, never knowing if he did or not.

Me and my health: Jim Davidson

Source: 'Me and my health: Jim Davidson talks to Graham Bridgstock', *Evening Standard*, 11 January 1994, p. 35

The main thing is I'm a constant worrier, a terrible panicker, convinced everything is going to go wrong (he confides before checking into an alcohol dependency clinic, having made his New Year's resolution to kick the booze for six months way back in October).

But then I do have a lot of responsibilities: I also run a multi-million-pound electronics company which hires out PA systems to rock bands and musicals. I invest in West End musicals ... Sometimes I just think I can't do all this: 'Please make them all go away, Mum. Just give me a cuddle and tell them to f*** off.'

Dad was an alcoholic and 79 when he died. He was a Scottish labourer, had two thirds of his stomach taken away during the war and everything wrong with him, asthma, bronchitis, pneumonia. He just ran out of life, couldn't even drink the whisky I bought him in the end.

Mum was Irish, from Cork. She was 74 when she died last year. That was lung cancer. They put her on steroids and I took her to see the panto I did at Wimbledon and Charlie Drake sat with her. When it happened he wrote me a lovely letter: 'Jim,' it said, 'sometimes the angels get lonely.'

It's weird. I still can't get used to the fact that she's gone. People ask me things and I say: 'Mum would know. I'll ask Mum.'

Looking back (as he does in his autobiography *The Full Monty*; Little, Brown, £14.99). I was overactive as a small boy and could read and write pretty well by the time I was four. But at nine or 10 I was hit in the eye by a stone from a catapult, it triggered a clot of blood behind the eye and I was blind for two weeks.

My Mum visited me at the Royal Eye Hospital at Elephant and Castle and offered one of her eyes to transplant, though my sight was eventually restored with special drugs and drops.

Born at home, sure, a council house at Kidbrooke, near Blackheath. No complications. It was like shelling peas. And I emerged to the strains of Debussy's *Claire de Lune* played by my Uncle Bill on the piano downstairs. To this day it's still the only tune I can play on the piano.

Breast-fed too. But no idea what I weighed at birth.

Now at 40 I'm 5ft 10in, and just under 13st. I was 11 when I started weight-training, hitting the old punchbag three times a week at the Imperial Hotel in Blackpool during the summer. And I put on a stone and a half, three inches on my chest, an inch on my biceps and took two inches off my waist.

My minder is a martial-arts expert. And I have some gym equipment in my back garden at home too (leafy Surrey, not far from Guildford). The trouble is I spent a fortune on shirts at Turnbull and Asser and I can't get into any of them now. And my suits don't fit any better.

Grey hair, yes. But I pick them out. And when I'm stressed I get the old dodgy scalp, a bit of dandruff.

My hearing's not good either. That's all the pyrotechnic effects on stage over the years. Now I tend to over-compensate for my lack of high frequency in one ear.

How old do I feel? Well, I think I've worn myself out a bit, burned the candle at both ends. I get tired, can't do the things I used to. If I have a late night it f***s me up for about three days.

But you can't tell an audience: 'I can't go on tonight. I've got flu,' or whatever. Instead you whack down a brandy and go on sniffing and hope Doctor Grease-paint takes over.

Ten years ago I went to a shrink for stage-fright. I was about 10 minutes into my act and I came off, felt terrible and threw up all over Lyn Paul, one of the Seekers. It was horrifying. I had these nightmares of not being able to cope on stage and then it was suddenly happening to me.

My second marriage had gone wrong. I had nowhere to live, no money and I'd turned into a nervous wreck. And this nice shrink told me I was using booze as a medicine and gave me some beta blockers for panic attacks.

Don't take them now. But I still keep one in the right-hand pocket of my stage trousers as a little comforter. And if I'm on a plane I always have one in my pocket then as well. The first thing I do on a plane, before I look at *High Life* or order a drink, is to find the sick bag.

Nerves make me throw up. I'm not scared of flying. It's crashing that I'm not too keen on. Then there's sitting on the plane for an hour. I just get panicky.

Vitamins, I take loads: royal jelly, ginseng, cod-liver oil, C, B, B12 shots every now and again, multi-vitamin injections, desiccated liver tablets ... Very health-conscious, true. I work at such a pace, drink too much, don't sleep enough and I'm always in a smoky environment, though I gave up cigarettes eight years ago. I was on 20 a day.

If I can't sleep I just have a drink. I can't sleep sober. I giggle in my sleep apparently, and grind my teeth. Some mornings I have a hangover you wouldn't believe. But I'm a drunk because I don't go to those meetings. You only have to go when you are an alcoholic. Drunks go to the pub.

Tracie (his fourth wife — he has five children) sleeps in the master bedroom. I sleep in the spare room. She likes lacy pillows and you'd turn over in the night and, if you hadn't shaved, the pillow would be hanging on to your face. Now I always throw pillows aside and sleep dead flat.

Tracie keeps herself fit and we've joined a new gym so we're going to train together. She's a great cook too. I like my food grilled because I'm making an effort to keep my cholesterol down by avoiding fat. Used to love steak tartare but I eat less red meat these days. I seem to have so much chicken I'm going to cluck soon.

When I had a medical for a mortgage the doctor said: 'Wee in this bottle.' So I weed into it, topped it up with tap water and gave it to him.

'Hmm. A little too much chlorine,' he said, holding it up to the light to examine it. I said: 'Well I have a swimming pool and I tend to swallow an awful lot of water.'

Broken bones? Only my right knuckle and left big toe. I dropped a paving slab on the toe and crushed it in my mother-in-law's garden a couple of wives ago.

And I broke my knuckle when my Dad was pissed and fighting my Mum. I grabbed hold of him and, to show him what I could do, punched the wall and unfortunately broke the bone. Then he hit me, put my spark out.

Any war-wounds sustained entertaining the troops in the Falklands, Beirut, Croatia and Bosnia? No, just clap in Germany in a whirlpool bath with a hooker: the condom must have floated off in the bubbles.

Me and my health: Maeve Haran

Source: 'Me and my health: Maeve Haran talks to Graham Bridgstock', *Evening Standard*, 23 August 1994, p. 27

Your boobs become very hot when you have a baby. The midwife gave me a wonderful tip. 'Wrap them in frozen cabbage leaves to keep them cool,' she said. And it works. The only trouble is, after a while you smell like goulash.

We had a period of infertility before I produced Georgia, seven, Holly, five, and Jimmy, seven months. You spend your life trying to avoid pregnancy as a career woman (she was editor of LWT's acclaimed *Six O'Clock Show*) and then, when you want to start a family, it doesn't happen. But we were lucky: there was none of the heartbreaking stuff.

Instead we had 18 months of bonking for babies, and none of it was wasted: it gave my partner (television producer Alex Graham) the idea for a drama series about infertility called *You, Me And It.*

Somebody pointed out that there was an erection in the first page of my latest book *It Takes Two* (Michael Joseph, £14.99): I hadn't noticed. The whole point about my books is they're about real life, the funny side, what it's like having children, trying to keep the passion going. I'm not the classic sex writer.

We were just about to go to Guy's Hospital to have some investigations done when I finally became pregnant. The last two were both born on 20 November, so I can economise on cards and parties.

Alex is my toyboy, a mere 40. We've been together for 14 years now. We're engaged, but wanted to be sure before we committed ourselves. Although I was 43 when Jimmy was born, I can recommend that highly.

You're more patient, though I don't much like the idea of being 63 when he's 20.

At 44 I feel exactly the same as I did when I was 19, but all my contemporaries look older. Mind you, I can't see my hand in front of me without glasses. And my memory? Well, I can't remember what I went downstairs for. Yet I can recall in glowing detail the appearance of a boy I went out with when I was 14.

At birth — in a nursing home in Worthing — I was the last of four children by five years. I think I was a mistake rather than an after-thought, but my parents took it on the chin.

Now I'm 5ft 7in with child-bearing hips, but do you have to ask me my weight? The answer is too much, to be honest about it. My daughters are going to be huge as well, tower over men and give them a hard time.

Ideally, I'd like a totally new body. Another four inches in the middle would do me, say Sigourney Weaver's body when she was Julia Roberts' age.

Sleep well? Yes, ever since I stopped working in television. We've just bought a 6ft bed. It's lovely. The mornings are really my favourite time when we're clambered over by all the children. Before they arrived we had lovely romantic picnics in bed. Nothing elaborate, just salady things, pork pies, lettuce, French bread, champagne. Now it's Ovaltine.

My parents were much-loved GPs in Worthing, Dr Tom and Dr Mary. The chaps went to him, the women to her. Both reached 63, then died within 12 months of each other. Mother had breast cancer, so I have to be careful because that's genetic, isn't it?

Father had irritable bowel syndrome and for the last 20 years of his life ate nothing but ham sandwiches and rice pudding. People put that down to Irish eccentricity, but I don't think it was. He just took the view that a bland diet was required. Kaolin and morphine were very much a smell of my childhood, too. He drank a lot of that, glug, glug, glug.

On the other hand, they were much less fussy than other people's parents. For example, when I was five and picked up a boiled sweet off the pavement and put it in my mouth, someone else's outraged mother said: 'Oh, how could you? It's disgusting!' And I replied: 'Oh, it's OK. My mother's a doctor and lets me do things like that.'

In Worthing we lived in a 20-roomed house, never had enough money and my mother did all the painting and decorating. My father wasn't a home handyman, though he was concerned to see that she didn't overdo things. 'That looks heavy,' he'd say. 'Why don't you make two journeys?'

Now I live in Highgate on the borders of Crouch End, or Couch End as the locals call it — there are so many shrinks there. I had therapy myself for years, saw a man three times a week, but stopped when I had Georgia.

The problem? I would call it lack of confidence, poor self-image. I did very well at school, but lost my nerve at university. It was a fear of being found out, that I wasn't as good as I wanted to be and other people thought I was.

It came from when I was a child really, probably inherited from my father's side. You know, melancholia. I just took a long time to build up confidence in myself.

What therapy can do is allow you to experience life instead of being scared of it. For years my father was frightened of death and never really enjoyed life.

Having children was the best thing that ever happened to me, my salvation. At last life made sense. As soon as I had them my perspective changed completely. Almost overnight I could see there was something more important than I was, and that's when I learned to count my blessings, to be happy. But it wasn't something that came spontaneously.

As a child I never had anything wrong with me except tonsils and wisdom teeth. The teeth were taken out at Worthing hospital when I was 11 or 12 and I tried to escape and was found, still under the anaesthetic, half-way down a corridor in my nightie. I avoid strenuously taking any form of exercise now, but in those days I spent my life at the swimming pool, yet never had a verruca though I always wanted one.

My two brothers, Tom and Patrick, both had them and I thought they sounded so glamorous. Somehow there was a sign of growing up in a verruca. At day school I assumed they were one of those things that just happened to you at boarding school.

However, my sister Rosaleen had something much more serious. That was polio, which left one of her legs shorter than the other, though you would never notice now. My mother didn't tell her till years later — she was afraid she might get a complex about it — and we all thought that was terribly wise.

Medical training myself? No. I'd call someone else in an emergency rather than me. I'm not at my best then. Take the day Holly had a pencil rubber stuck up her nose. I was hopeless, in a complete panic.

'Oh God, we've got to go to Casualty,' I said. But my 19-year-old nanny strode up quite calmly, put a finger over Holly's other nostril and said: 'Blow!' — and down it came.

Me and my health: Virginia Ironside

Source: 'Me and my health: Virginia Ironside talks to Graham Bridgstock', *Evening Standard*, 21 June 1994, p. 45

My mother had a couple of face-lifts, but I don't think I'm quite into that yet, though I have been on HRT for three months. At 50, I feel a mixture of 65 and eight, sometimes mature and confident, sometimes like a kid with my thumb in my mouth.

A short-sighted kid, of course. I've always worn glasses, which makes swimming a bit of a drag: I can't see the end of the pool. Not that I give a pin about exercise. Why walk when you can drive? That's what I do all the time.

Actually, I don't take any special care of myself. Yet I seldom get colds or flu. And at 5ft 7in I'm 10st and eat as much butter and cream as I like and my cholesterol level is ace.

Food faddism is so annoying. Even my son Will, 20, examines the sell-by date on yoghurt, When I was brought up, if there was fur on it you didn't put it in the bin. You removed the fur and ate the rest. No doubt I'm so full of bacteria now there's very little that can get a grip on me.

All I can say is, when I was in Egypt I was the only one going to the Valley of Kings confident that all would be well. Everyone was afraid to stray far from a lavatory. Naturally, I sympathised: I've suffered from ulcerative colitis for 25 years and, when you're in crisis mode, you can be accident-prone.

People who lay down the law about smoking in their homes can also be irritating. 'My flat is a smokeless zone,' they say.

I've given up now. But sometimes when I hear that, I'm tempted to start again.

Meanwhile, I love to see others light up at meal times.

My father smoked like a chimney. My partner Denis smokes. And I like the smell of smoke in the house (terraced property in Shepherd's Bush which they share with two cats, Corky and Gums — hence her latest book *Goodbye, Dear Friend: Coming to Terms with the Death of a Pet*, Robson, £11.95).

Cats are very relaxing, though Gums thinks my ear lobes are his mother's boobs and sucks them.

An Aquarian, yes, and like Will an only child, which is not much fun. He enjoys life, is studying social anthropology at Manchester and plays the ukulele in a band. Everyone I've ever been romantically involved with has been an Aquarian — my ex-husband, my partner, and all the people in between.

I don't see the doctor often, though my GP did refer me to a specialist not long ago when my face came out in spots. 'Middle-aged acne,' said the dermatologist, and put me on a low dose of antibiotics. They disappeared in a couple of months.

Now I feel like going up to people with spots in the street and telling them the good news — there are drugs these days that can cure the worst cases.

I can identify with even the odder problems: I can't bear being in a restaurant surrounded by dying plants myself, have to get up and pour Perrier water on them.

But, offhand, I don't know that there are any health hazards to being an Agony Aunt. It makes me feel better not worse.

First, in the sense that I can help people. And being an Agony Aunt (now with *Today* and *The Independent*) does give you access to a lot of information which seems to be kept from others.

Men write: 'I'm having a prostate operation. Will I ever be able to make love again?' Nobody's told them.

And second, however low you feel, you can't be quite as low as some people who write in. In a pile of letters there may be half-a-dozen from people who want to kill themselves.

My own mother (Professor Janey Ironside, head of fashion at the Royal College of Art during the Sixties) tried to commit suicide twice with pills. She was an alcoholic, left home when I was 14.

She had breast cancer which spread, couldn't have been more than 63 when she died, yet she was pleased to go. She'd stopped drinking by then but was very depressed, living on tranquillisers and biscuits. It was very sad. She was so gifted, successful, funny and a delightful woman in a way — but not a real mum.

On the other hand, my father (the equally distinguished artist Christopher Ironside) reached 79. He went into hospital on the Thursday with suspected thrombosis and on the Saturday they told him he had leukaemia and that chemotherapy would start on the Monday. But, being sensible, he turned his head to the wall on the Sunday night and didn't wake up, which I think was absolutely right. He had glaucoma as well, was losing his sight and, if he'd hung on, his life would have been a misery.

That's when the depression that I've been lumbered with on and off since I was a child came back. Everything happened at the same time. I was sacked by the *Sunday Mirror*. And I'd been in the throes of the menopause as well.

Mine is classic depression. You feel better in the evening, though even then it's as if you're somehow detached, as if there was a pane of glass between you and the rest of the world.

Over the years there isn't much I haven't tried: pills, shrinks, counsellors, group therapy ... However, it's only recently I've felt I'm beginning to get the measure of it.

People might read this and think: 'So how come she's an Agony Aunt?' But, in fact, being depressed makes you ideally qualified because you spend your entire life trying to find out the answers and on the way acquire a great deal of wisdom. And, while wisdom doesn't necessarily make you happy, it does mean you become quite an expert on the subject.

So I don't feel a fraud, though I realise some people would say: 'If you're an Agony Aunt you should have got it all sorted out by now.'

Alas, I haven't yet. But I am trying all the time.

Whether it's because I was brought up by an alcoholic mother who was depressed or whether it's a genetic thing I don't know. A bit of both, I should think.

Either way I was a shy, gloomy, tearful child looked after when I was tiny by au pairs. I had two, one German, one French. They each did a year, then left and I never saw them again. What I felt at the time I don't know. But I do suffer a lot of anxiety now about people going away.

Which is why when I had Will I resolved, come hell or high water, I would never have a nanny. And when I was bringing him up it put the depression on hold for a while.

When you're depressed you want someone to look after you, and looking after someone else is almost as good because you're involved in the process of caring. If you build a fire for a freezing man, some of the heat comes your way, too.

There are great troughs of insecurity in everyone, I believe. Even Cecil King, who was an amusing and successful man, told me he longed to die and that every time he went up in an aeroplane he hoped it would crash.

'Life is like trying to wade through treacle,' he said.

Me and my health: Lynda La Plante

Source: 'Me and my health: Lynda La Plante talks to Graham Bridgstock', *Evening Standard*, 16 July 1993, p. 43

Breastfed, yes, and I was potty-trained exceedingly early, too, and took rather an obsessive interest in it. My poor mother would be in the middle of a cocktail party and I would suddenly appear, po in hand, acknowledging everybody in the room like royalty, and sit down and do the business.

Then when I'd finished I would pull up my little knickers and, po in hand again, make my exit to a round of applause.

According to my mother I was like the cat. I brought in everything — mumps, measles, scarlet fever, chickenpox — and gave it to my younger sister Gilly, who always got it 20 times worse than I did. Take chickenpox. I had two spots. She had so many you couldn't put a pinpoint between them.

It's a good job dyslexia isn't catching: I had to have special help for that at school and later at RADA. Otherwise I wouldn't have been able to read scripts, never mind learn my lines.

In my acting days I was a walking danger zone as well, because whenever they had a blackout between scenes I was incapable of finding my way into the wings.

The curtain would go up again and there I'd be centre stage, saying: 'I'm awfully sorry!' and scuttling off.

Now conjunctivitis is the problem when I'm perched at my computer all day writing TV series and books (for her latest see *Entwined*, Pan, £4.99). That's Mother Nature saying: 'Excuse me. Don't wear out your eyeballs. You've only got two.' The specialist I consulted said: 'You must stop working so hard.'

And he has a point. I know it's stupid to push myself to exhaustion the way I do. The trouble is I don't notice it until it's too late.

Nothing ever stops me. Like yesterday. I got up at 6.30 and had breakfast — fresh-squeezed orange juice, black coffee with Hermesetas, fresh fruit and bran cereal, or roughage as my mother calls it. Then I started work and didn't stop till 10pm.

No wonder I'm half a stone overweight. Not enough exercise. I should really be eight stone.

Sure, we have our own heated pool at home in Kingston upon Thames. But somehow I only associate swimming with holidays.

I've also done the aerobic scene, even had a one-to-one trainer. She used to get right up my nose, laughed if I fell over and I thought: She'll have to go.

Then there's stodge. I love homely fattening food. Show me a sponge pudding with syrup and custard and it's like a magnet. It's the same with cream crackers and lashings of butter or eggs and bacon, sausage, black pudding and fried bread.

Don't know what I weighed at birth. All I know is I made my first appearance in Warrington at midnight on 15 March — the Ides of March — and I was crying from the word go, had open tear ducts.

There were four in the family. My sister Dale died at the age of five. Then there's Gilly, who's a TV casting director, and my brother Michael, who's a GP in Yorkshire and 6ft 4in.

We had a tall granny, too — Granny Southwood, who lived to 94 and never bothered with doctors.

'Give me a bottle of Guinness and I'll be all right,' she'd say.

A good patient, yes. I'll take anything anybody gives me if I'm not well. I had a lump in my left breast removed and one in my groin, both benign, but I still keep a close watch.

Of course everything that happens to me is a farce. The first one was a rush job. I coughed, found the lump and was in within 24 hours.

The ward was mainly for lumps, benign or malignant, though there was one patient who kept saying: 'I'm only here for my varicose veins. I don't want them taking anything away.'

Presently a doctor came in and said: 'Could you tell me where your lump is please?'

I said: 'Yes, here.' Then he drew a circle round the spot on my breast with a blue felt-tip pen. And he was followed at intervals by two other doctors on the same mission. The first drew a cross on the spot with a green felt-tip pen, the second a square with a red one.

Finally the surgeon arrived, took one look and chuckled. 'Good heavens!' he said. 'Who's been playing noughts and crosses?'

Next they wanted me to sign to say if they found anything malignant they could operate immediately.

But I said: 'No, I won't sign.'

And this woman said: 'What d'you mean, you won't sign?'

I said: 'If I'm having my breast removed I want to be in a place of peace and quiet, not a noisy public ward.'

The woman said: 'But I've never had anyone not sign before ...'

Then the patient in the next bed said: 'Well, if she's not signing, I'm not either!'

That was in London eight years ago. The groin was two or three years earlier in New Mexico. I was in terrific pain then and they decided to operate without delay. But the surgeon didn't speak a word of English. So his assistant filled in the forms instead.

He said: 'How tall are you?'

I said: '5 (ft) 2 (in).'

And in the space reserved for Age he duly wrote 52 and then said: 'You don't look it.'

In fact, I'm 47 now, though I never acknowledge it normally. Sometimes I feel 25, sometimes — when I look in the mirror — 70. Then I think: Oh God, the old bat!

That's why I fully intend to have everything lifted, the whole lot done, eyes, lips ... I have lines at the top of my lips and I would like those whipped off for a start. And my husband, American screenwriter Richard La Plante, is encouraging me.

Sadly we have no children, though I took fertility drugs for three years.

At the clinic I went up to the doctor and said: 'Do we have sex before we come in or after?'

He said: 'Well, I should think you should do it the morning you come in — but I'm only the hall porter.'

Richard's a fitness freak, into Kung Fu and he boxes and works out in the gym. He has to. He feels physically ill if he doesn't exercise. We're both restless sleepers so we have a huge bed, or rather two large single beds put together.

Tallulah, our Irish wolfhound, is not allowed upstairs. If a dog that size came up and lay on the bed she would flatten you.

First-aid training, no. I was in the Brownies but only for four hours so I never got round to it. Actually I'd only got my uniform and done a few dib-dibs when a friend said: 'I bet you can't tap-dance on that drum.' I said: 'Bet I can.'

And I went straight through it and that was me and the Brownies finished.

Naturally my parents took it all in their stride. Father's 85 now and was very active, played tennis, cricket and golf. Then he had a hip-replacement operation and it's slowed him down a bit.

Mother always swore by syrup of figs when we were kids. She's certainly a good advertisement for it now, so lively. She's 83 and she's just learned to swim.

Guess I take after her. Put it this way. I'm not a robust person. But I'm resilient.

Me and my health: Claire Tomalin

Source: 'Me and my health: Claire Tomalin talks to Graham Bridgstock', *Evening Standard*, 25 October 1994, p. 39

Physical jerks? Yes, occasionally. Years ago I read a newspaper feature headed 'Make yourself a goddess'. There were four exercises and all you had to do was 10 of each every day.

Even now, at 61, when I think I'm in danger of not looking goddess like, I do those for a bit (says the prize-winning biographer, sipping mineral water in the shade of a fig tree in her Camden Town garden, after putting the finishing touches to her latest book *Mrs Jordan's Profession*, Viking, £18).

I was a dreamy child; I've always been pretty vague. That's partly connected with being short-sighted, I think.

There is something to be said for short-sightedness, however: short-sighted women are kinder than women with perfect sight, I believe. We see the world through this faint blur and the defects of other people are slightly blotted out.

My parents both took a lot of exercise; otherwise, they were extremely moderate. Neither of them smoked. My mother permitted herself perhaps one glass of sherry a year, and Father drinks very little.

I grew up entirely without medicines; I never had Aspirins and I'm still reluctant to take one.

My mother was a Christian Scientist and this is a tremendous advantage in life because I was brought up to believe that one wasn't ill. Mother made light of all ailments, though I can remember her being rather angry with me once because I vomited.

She had my elder sister, Marguerite, in a grand nursing home and, to her horror, they gave her an anaesthetic. So she insisted on having me at home in St Peter's Square, Chiswick: she was just lying down after lunch, gave one heave and out I came.

That was on 20 June, 1933. I weighed 7lb and everything went smoothly, though the doctor scolded my mother for not sending for him sooner.

She was a composer, eight years older than my father. He worked for the United Nations, is 89 this month and until two years ago was walking up mountains.

My mother was 87 when she died; that was Alzheimer's disease. Michael (her playwright husband Michael Frayn, also 61) and I have a pact. I said to him: 'If I start getting like that, will you give me a pill to finish me off?'

He said: 'Well, you're getting very forgetful already.' He has a point: sometimes I go upstairs to fetch something, then can't remember what it was. Yet I'm naturally optimistic. I tend to wake up every morning thinking: 'Hooray, a new day!'

I think if I did develop some frightful disease, I might not fight it very hard. I mean, I have already had 61 good years. I've always been easy about my age and slightly mystified by women who worry about theirs. I adored being 30 and looked forward to being a formidable old woman.

Not that I live the way you're supposed to live in your sixties. For example, I still bicycle around the district — to the hairdressers, that sort of thing — despite having broken a collar-bone and hit my head when I came off 10 years ago; the brake became entangled in the back wheel and I flew through the air, but managed to crawl home.

See the doctor often? No, though I owe her a great debt. Not for my health — she regards me as odiously healthy — but for what she has done for my son, Tom, who was born with spina bifida 24 years ago.

People may think: 'Poor Tom ... in a wheelchair.' But he starred in a television film, has an A-level in French and travels by himself. He has just spent a week in the mountains in France with his grandfather.

The doctor and I are the same age and I realise with horror that she will retire just when I need her. Still, apart from colds and flu, I'm never ill.

Michael's back goes out from time to time, which is painful. However, he's very stoical. It's his height — he's 6ft 1in, and the kindest man imaginable.

But he's a very bad patient. He hates being ill; he won't go to bed, just sits up in his chair, and I fuss like mad. I'm very fortunate in my second marriage.

Nick (her first husband, journalist Nicholas Tomalin, who was killed in 1973 while reporting the Yom Kippur war) and I had a stormy marriage.

The mother-in-law/daughter-in-law relationship is a difficult one, and in the early stages we were quite suspicious of each other. She (Nick's mother) thought I didn't appreciate her son; I thought she spoiled Nick. But we came to love each other very much.

She was a psychiatric social worker and said: 'Why don't you and Nick have some counselling?' At first I was resistant to the idea, though I went to see a woman the Tavistock Centre sent me to and never regretted it. She was lovely, very wise and sensible.

'We're not going to have anything like analysis. We will just talk every week for a few months,' she said. It was more like mother and daughter, and she helped me stick up for myself.

We married on the basis that we wanted six children. That was in 1955, when no one ever thought about the world being over-populated. Well, we didn't. (They had five — two sons and three daughters, though Daniel survived only a month and Susanna, who suffered from depression, took her own life at the age of 22.)

When Daniel died, I determined, like falling off a horse, to have another baby immediately and Emily was born on his birthday a year later. Emily was my mother's name and my grandmother's.

The worst thing I had as a child was a mastoid infection when I was four. It can't have been easy for my mother. One surgeon at the homoeopathic hospital said: 'If we operate on this, the child will die.' Another said: 'If we don't operate, she will die.'

In the end, they didn't and, in due course, I recovered. I shall always be grateful to a lovely nurse there who read Beatrix Potter's *The Tale of Tom Kitten* to me. I later read it to my children and to granddaughter Rosa, who is seven, and I could still recite it to you now.

Me and my health: Sir Peregrine Worsthorne

Source: 'Me and my health: Sir Peregrine Worsthorne talks to Graham Bridgstock', *Evening Standard*, 24 May 1994, p. 26

My mother was worried: I was 15 and abnormally small for my age. But she had a friend, a Dr Gurevitch, who specialised in injections to make you grow. God knows what they were. Maybe they were risky. Maybe she was imprudent, putting my fate in his hands. But she admired him greatly, he was the brother of Eleanor Roosevelt's doctor in America.

So she took me to see him in London. I went up from boarding school in the country. It gave me a day out and I was happy to have it because it meant missing compulsory games. And obviously it did the trick. The transformation was miraculous. I shot up like Jack and the Beanstalk.

My parents were both very small, though not midgets. And my brother, Simon, who didn't have the Gurevitch treatment is 5ft 5in. He's 72 now, Lord Lieutenant of Lancashire, and was knighted in the last New Year Honours, so he has caught up with me at last.

Whereas I'm 70, 6ft and about 11st. Weight originally? No idea. All I know is I was born at home in Cadogan Square and I think I was punctual, though that was the last time I was for anything.

According to my mother I was nearly always antagonistic 'even at the breast'. It conjures up a terrible picture: a nibbling angry infant.

But looking back (as he does in his autobiography, *Tricks Of Memory*, Weidenfeld and Nicolson, £18.99), I have had only one long period in hospital.

That was with jaundice when I was 25. I was in St Thomas's for four months, turned canary yellow and went down to under 7st. I was so emaciated I looked like someone from Auschwitz. I thought I was a goner. So did they.

After a while you adapt to illness being normal and health being abnormal. One almost didn't like visitors. They wanted to talk about what was going on in the outside world. And all I wanted to talk about was what was going on in the hospital.

Nothing occupied my waking — and, indeed, my dreaming — hours more than the colour of my urine. The darker the yellow froth, the worse I was getting, the lighter, the better. Otherwise you just lie on your back and hope for the best. There's no treatment, not even diet.

'Eat whatever you like,' they said. And that is what I did. One afternoon my mother was horrified to find me gnawing at a wing of grouse from a Fornum and Mason hamper my father had brought me. They were divorced by then and she disapproved, arrived bearing fruit and rusks herself.

How did I get jaundice in the first place? That is what I asked the doctor.

He said: 'Well, one of the ways — which can't possibly affect you, Mr Worsthorne — is rats.'

Of course I didn't say: 'It probably affects me more than anybody else in London.' Yet it was true. I had just got married and we were living in a little house on the South Bank opposite St Paul's Cathedral.

The property — which belonged to the Swedish writer Axel Munthe, author of *The Story Of San Michele* — was right by the river and infested by rats from the barges. They actually crawled up the covers of our four-poster, though the local ratcatchers — two old Cockney women — were very taken with them. 'The little dears!' they'd say.

The last time I saw the doctor, however, was at the New Year for psittacosis. The symptoms are like flu, high temperature, aching limbs, lack of energy ... I thought it was flu. So did he at first.

At one point I had a temperature of 104 — the highest I've ever had in my life — and I thought he would be impressed. But no. Unlike matron at school, he never takes your temperature.

It dragged on and in the end I went to a specialist who, after some blood tests, said: 'Have you had any contact with parrots?'

And the answer was yes. When my wife (Lady Lucinda Lambton, 20 years his junior and wife No 2) launched her book on animals a lot of exotic birds were invited to the party; including several performing parrots. One of them, a trained roller-skater, nipped me on the arm, though that was a year ago now.

'It may have been lying dormant since,' the specialist pointed out.

Psittacosis is still quite rare and has been fatal in the past, though it's treatable now, I'm glad to say, and he put me on tetracyclines. But it was all of two months before I felt better.

Good patient? No. I'm a bad-tempered, querulous impatient patient. I do what I'm told, but with bad grace.

Constipation is my Achilles heel. I first had it at school. The army was hell, too, because the facilities were so awful.

But I don't want to exaggerate. I've never consulted a doctor about it. Instead I take Potters Little Liver Pills — not every day, but as necessary.

It's fine at home (Victorian rectory, rural Buckinghamshire). But if I'm away it can be a problem though, unlike most people who get diarrhoea in India, the food there gives me the regular movements you're supposed to have.

War wounds? No. Only a dislocated shoulder on an army assault course when I was a platoon commander in the Ox and Bucks. They made you climb these artificial stone walls and drop down on the over side. Unfortunately, I fell on my shoulder and put it out very badly, even dropped my glass when the CO proposed the Loyal Toast in the officers' mess and was laid up for three months.

If your parents have lived a long time you have a better chance, don't you? So I'm lucky. My mother had a stroke at 90 but lived to 92. And my father reached 90. According to the post-mortem he had cancer. At 70 the good news is I've been taking a pill for gout every day for five years and haven't had a twinge since.

Inevitably I feel less able to run a mile or climb a stile but I walk the dogs (two dachshunds, two mongrels) and swim at Cliveden, which is round the corner from us. They have an indoor and an outdoor pool — the outdoor is the Christine Keeler one.

Everything is still in working order, though I suppose less active than in the prime of life. But then I have never been very physical and I've had a pretty sedentary life. So declining powers don't constitute a tremendous source of misery because I didn't take advantage of them when I had them. On the other hand, I wouldn't mind my libido taking a turn for the better. But that is something which tends to decline from the age of 21.

While my eyesight is better than it was, my memory is worse. Not long ago somebody asked me what the Gunpowder Plot was about and I couldn't remember. It's embarrassing. I'm also asked to appear on talk programmes and whereas I used to have no difficulty remembering why I thought something now I have completely forgotten.

However, I don't lose any sleep over it. On the contrary. I drop off the moment my head hits the pillow and it's an awful thing to admit, but I average eight hours. According to Napoleon no adult worth their salt needs more than five hours and I daresay I don't need them, but I certainly have them.

We have a Victorian four-poster and I wear cotton pyjamas from Marks and Spencer. No, I don't wear a nightcap, though I had a friend, a Lithuanian émigré, who used to say he couldn't sleep without a hairnet, and he wasn't homosexual.

Acknowledgements

Grateful acknowledgement is made to the following sources for permission to reproduce material in this unit:

Text

Brody, H. (1987) *Stories of Sickness*, Yale University Press, copyright © 1987 by Yale University. All rights reserved; Parker, G. (1991) 'They've got their own lives to lead: carers and dependent people talking about family and neighbourhood help', in Hutton, J. et al (eds) *Dependency to Enterprise*, Routledge; 'Me and my health: Dianne Abbott talks to Graham Bridgstock', *Evening Standard*, 22nd February 1994; 'Me and my health: Jeff Banks talks to Graham Bridgstock', *Evening Standard*, 12th April 1994; 'Me and my health: Max Bygraves talks to Graham Bridgstock', *Evening Standard*, 23rd April 1993; 'Me and my health: Jim Davidson talks to Graham Bridgstock', *Evening Standard*, 11th January 1994; 'Me and my health: Maeve Haran talks to Graham Bridgstock', *Evening Standard*, 23rd August 1994; 'Me and my health: Virginia Ironside talks to Graham Bridgstock', *Evening Standard*, 21st June 1994; 'Me and my health: Lynda La Plante talks to Graham Bridgstock', *Evening Standard*, 16th July 1993; 'Me and my health: Claire Tomalin talks to Graham Bridgstock', *Evening Standard*, 25th October 1994; 'Me and my health: Sir Peregrine Worsthorne talks to Graham Bridgstock', *Evening Standard*, 24th May 1994;

Photos

p. 15, p. 35, p. 44 , p. 46, p. 99: Sally & Richard Greenhill; p. 18: Universal Pictorial Press; p. 87: BBC Photo Library, with the kind permission of Trevor Peacock and Dona Croll, and of Scott Marshall Personal Management and of Hamper Neafsey.

Cover illustration

Kasimir Malevich, *Sportsmen*, c.1928–32, oil on canvas, 142x164, State Russian Museum, St Petersburg.